CW00408383

Maurizio Sansone MD

Clinical allergy and immunology specialist

www.mauriziosansone.it
info@mauriziosansone.it

Graphics: Andrea Errigo

Word processing: Dr. Anita Vecchioli MD

Edutor: Carli Williams

. Maurizio Sansone MD

Nikel-free Cooking

Tips and recipes for people with nickel allergies

Table of Contents

8 Preface

10 The basics of allergies

14 Nickel, the stranger

15 Contact dermatitis

17 The allergy to nickel sulphate

19 SNAS

21 A low nickel diet

26 Risks of the nickel-free diet

28 Factors influencing nickel absorption

31 The epicutaneous test, also known as the patch test

33 The correlation between celiac disease and nickel allergies

35 Contact reactions to foods

37 Food intolerances: fake news or reality?

39 Clinical Cases

45 Appetizers

Buttered anchovies - Bruschetta - Salmon carpaccio - Shrimp cocktail - Sea bass bruschetta –Cream frites - Seafood salad - Sea bass paté- Codfish balls - Ham and melon - Stuffed rusks - Sautéed clams - Smoked kebabs - Ground kebabs

60 First courses

Arancini di riso - Neapolitan Calzone - Cannelloni with ricotta cheese and spinach - Fettuccine with meat sauce - Gnocchi with gorgonzola - Gricia pasta - Mezze with tuna - Ricotta soup - Broccoli orecchiette - Paccheri with calamari - Pasta with oven – Four cheese penne pasta - Penne with cooked ham - Penne with ricotta - Penne with saffron - Penne with salmon and saffron - Pennette with vodka – Four cheese pizza - Pizza with croutons – Capricciosa pizza - Pizza with carbonara - Ravioli with ricotta - Rigatoni with lemon - Rigatoni with sausage and cream - Lying rice - Veal risotto - Smoked risotto - Risotto with castelmagno – Orange risotto - Risotto with - Risotto with Milanese style - Risotto with risotto – Seafood risotto - Risotto with black sauce - Spaghetti with garlic and olive oil - Spaghetti alla provolone - Spaghetti alla bottarga - Spaghetti alla carbonara - Spaghetti with clams Tagliolini with sea bass - Tortellini - soup patatea

103 Main dishes

Fried lamb - Lamb chops - Baked lamb - Baked anchovies - Orange duck in the microwave - Pork loin with milk - Braciato - Bourguignonne meat - Beef carpaccio - Salmon carpaccio - Baked lamb roast leg - Mussels with marinara sauce - Marsala slices - Cod fillets - Beef fillet in butter - Beef fillet in salt - Valdostana fondue - Breaded cheese - Ham frittata – Mixed fried fish - Fish of the poor - Seafood salad - Octopus salad - Tuna rice salad - Rolls - American rolls - Beef boiled meat - Lard in the microwave - Baked pork with apples - Baked meat - Omelette stuffed - Ossobuchi alla Milanese - Grilled swordfish - Chicken breast with lemon - Chicken breast with wine - Chicken cacciatore - Chicken Marengo - Boneless chicken - Fried chicken - Meatballs in the pan - Meatballs impanate - Veal roulade - Sausages with roast potatoes - Saltimbocca alla romana - Grilled scamorza - Mogliia sole - Beer stew - Meat skewers - Sea bass - Meat tartare - Tuna tartar - Bolognese tortellini - Eggs with bacon - Boiled eggs with cheese - Boiled eggs with ham - Boiled eggs with truffles - Boiled eggs with tuna - Boiled eggs with prawns - Boiled eggs with sausage- Scrambled eggs with ham - Veal tonnato

164 Side dishes

Potato bombs - Cacioimperio - Potato croquettes – Boiled potatos - Potatoes and bacon- Mashed potatoes - Ricotta au gratin - Potato pie

173 Desserts and sweets

Bananas flambé - Cream puffs - Fig biscuits - Creme caramel – Crepes with butter and sugar - Fruit tart without cooking - Fruit tart - Sweet chestnut fruit tart - Sponge cake - Panna cotta - American cake - Apple pie with ricotta – Apple cake- Apple and cheese cake - Tartar soup

Preface

The author's goal is to provide both scientific and practical information on the different types of nickel allergies, which affect between 9 and 13% of the global population (percentages varying between 9 and 13% of the population with a clear prevalence of the female gender). There are two types of nickel allergies.

1. Contact dermatitus (DAC): the classic contact dermatitis that occurs due to contact with the skin;
2. Systemic nickel allergy syndrome (SNAS): the dietary form that affects the entire body

A patient can experience symptoms from both types of the allergy, either seperately or in conjunction. Since this allergy's symptoms not only occur via physical contact, but also through ingestion of substances containing high nickel content, this book is equipped with many tasty "nickel-free" recipes to support those who have difficulties finding risk-free food options.

The basics of allergies

To understand the conept of allergies and possible therapies and prevention strategies, it is important to learn about the protagonist of the allergic reaction, the allergen. Allergens are antigens which are substances recognized as foreign by the immune system. Due to the characteristics of the antigen, this introduction of an antigen can lead to an allergic reaction by contact, ingestion, inhalation, exposure, or inoculation. To summarize, an allergic reaction is a particular type of immunologic response that the human body produces in reaction to specific heterologous substances.

In general, when our body encounters a foreign substance, the immune system acts much like that of any countries "customs". In fact, all substances present a series of antigens, which the human body's immune system groups into one of two categories: 1) "self", that which is belonging to the organism and, 2) "non-self", that which is foreign.

If the substance introduced into the body is recognized as "non-self", the immune system, through the production of antibodies (IgA, IgG IgE and IgM class immunoglobulins) and specific cells, will try to eliminate the "danger". Not all substances have antigens on the surface. In fact, only high molecular weight proteins can induce an immune response, unlike sugars and amino acids which have low molecular weights or "linear" structures. Proteins, which you already may know, are the basis of all organic structures. They are also on the surface of viruses and bacteria as proof of the fundamental role of the recognition of "self" and "non-self" in protecting us from infections. When we ingest a protein through food consumption, it is broken down into its basic components, the amino acids, before being assimilated. In this way the proteins, both animal and vegetable, that are taken with the diet do not risk inducing an antibody response. Furthermore, our digestive system has a barrier to prevent proteins from entering circulation.

According to the original classification by Gell and Coombs, the abnormal immunological reactions are of four types:

1. immediate reaction type (or anaphylaxis);
2. cytotoxic type;
3. type of immune complex;
4. cell-mediated type.

Type 1 and 4 reactions (immediate and cell-mediated) relate to the typical allergic immune response.

Immediate reaction or anaphylaxis

Some individuals are genetically predisposed to allergies. The bodies are such people produce antibodies (of the IgE series) in response to some external agents. These antibodies are different from those that non-allergic subjects produce. Now let's see what happens when our allergic patient takes a walk in a park in the middle of spring. The pollen, abundantly present in the atmosphere, is inhaled. The immune system recognizes it as "non-self" and produces antibodies of the IgE series. At this point it is necessary to make a chemical clarification to understand structure of these antibodies. They are shaped roughly like the letter "Y". With the two upper arms they attach themselves to the external agent, while with the lower arm they weld themselves to the wall of specific cells of our organism called "mast cells". These cells are rich in histamine. Let us look at an example. When two IgE immunoglobulins, which have reacted with an external pollen, are next to each other, they change their chemical structure. With the arm attached to the mast, they pierce the cell wall. This leads to the leakage of the contents of the mast cell, that is, histamines, which induces vasodilation and then edema (swelling). This is the the allergic reaction in practice. What has happened in this example corresponds to the first type of reaction, the one defined as immediate.

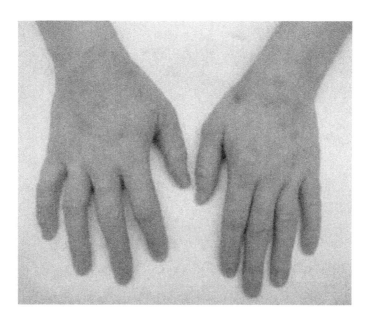

The cell-mediated reaction

The intermediaries of the cell-mediated immunological response are the lymphocytes. The cellular response of our body is mainly, but not only, connected to intracellular pathogens. A typical example is that of tuberculosis. At first contact with the extraneous agent, the lymphocytes (CD4 +) bind to the antigen and are transformed over a couple of days into

sensitized lymphocytes (TH1). Our organism's next contact with the antigen will provoke an activation of the TH1 lymphocyte. This involves the release of toxic substances from the cell which are able to fight the foreign agent. The on-site presence of toxic substances provokes evident tissue damage (eczema) which is manifested by cutaneous infiltration, redness, swelling, itching and sometimes small lacerations of the skin. This is what happens, for example, when contact occurs with nickel. Thus, contact dermatitis is a typical example of the cell-mediated reaction.

Perivascular leukocyte clusters are essential for efficient activation of effector T cells in the skin. Natsuaki Y., Egawa G., Nakamizo S., Ono S., Hanakawa S., Okada T., Kusuba N., Otsuka A., Ki- toh A., Honda T., Nakajima S., Tsuchiya S., Sugimoto Y., Ishii K.J., Tsutsui H., Yagita H., Iwakura Y., Kubo M., Ng L.G., Hashimoto T., Fuentes J., Guttman-Yassky E., Miyachi Y., Kabashima K. Nat Immunol. 2014 Nov; 15(11):1064-9.

Contact Hypersensitivity.
Gaspari A.A., Katz S.I., Martin S.F.
Curr Protoc Immunol. 2016 Apr 1; 113:4.2.1-7.

Contact dermatitis considerations in atopic dermatitis. Rundle C.W., Bergman D., Goldenberg A., Jacob S.E. Clin Dermatol. 2017 Jul–Aug; 35(4):367-374.
The role and relevance of mast cells in urticaria. Church M.K., Kolkhir P., Metz M., Maurer M. Immunol Rev. 2018 Mar; 282(1):232-247.

Nickel, the stranger

Nickel is a natural element discovered in 1757 by the chemist Cronestedt. Its atomic weight is 28 and it has 5 isotopes. This element is ubiquitous and is found mostly in igneous rocks, often linked with iron. The earth's crust is made up of 0.008% nickel. More specifically, in the soil we find 5-500 µg / g, in plants 0.5-5 µg / g, in the animal kingdom 0.1-5 µg / g, in water 0.0005-0.0010 µg / g .

To avoid the common confusion between nickel and iron it is important to emphasize that iron, also a chemical element, is different from nickel. Nickel is a ferromagnetic element. In nature it is often found associated with cobalt and is used in alloys for its properties.

The largest nickel reserves are in Australia and New Caledonia and amount to about 50% of total known reserves. Nevertheless, Russia is a the large nickel producer with around 20% of the world's production and is closely followed by Canada, Australia, Indonesia and the Philippines.

A great advantage of nickel is its ability to resist oxidation. Therefore, it is used to make coins, laboratory instruments, commonly used cutlery, and pipes.

In human biology, nickel contributes to numerous enzyme reactions necessary for cellular activity.

Our body's intake of nickel occurs mainly through oral consumption and, to a lesser extent, through respiration and skin contact. When consumed orally, nickel is almost eliminated in an unchanged state through feces. Instead, the metal absorbed through respiration or skin contact is exclusively eliminated via urine. Consequently, there is no toxic nickel accumulation in the general population except for those whose work puts them in daily contact with large quantities of this metal.

Relationship between nickel allergy and diet. Sharma A.D.Indian J Dermatol Venereol Leprol. 2007 Sep–Oct; 73(5):307–12.

Trace metal metabolism in plants. Andresen E., Peiter E., Küpper H. J Exp Bot. 2018 Feb 13.

Sensitization to nickel: etiology, epidemiology, immune reactions, prevention, and therapy. Hostynek J.J.Rev Environ Health. 2006 Oct–Dec; 21(4):253-80.

Minerals in foods: dietary sources, chemical forms, interactions, bioavailability. Hazell T.World Rev Nutr Diet. 1985; 46:1–123.

Contact dermatitis

Contact dermatitis, as the name suggests, is a dermatologic manifestation caused by contact with certain chemical substances. At the foundation of contact dermatitis there is an abnormal reaction in the body involving certain white blood cells called lymphocytes. The clinical form manifests itself through:

- erythema (redness of the skin);

- intense itching;

- edema (swelling of the skin).

Unlike urticaria, which manifests itself through welts that can last just a few hours or even through lesions that last several days.

In the field of contact dermatitis there are two types: the "professional" form and a "common" form". The first form relates to contact with chemical substances with uncommon uses. Therefore, it usually affects workers in particular sectors including construction, welding, plumbing, electricity, and cosmotology. The second type concerns contact with commonly used substances and therefore can affect anyone.

There are numerous types of dermatitis caused by contact with rubber, metals, detergents, cosmetics, perfumes, and much more. For obvious reasons, the most affected areas are the hands, but any part of the body can be affected through the use of cosmetics, detergents, and so on.

All contact dermatitis nickel sulphate allergies are distinguished by both frequency and symptomatology.

Contact dermatitis: facts and controversies.
Wolf R., Orion E., Ruocco E., Baroni A., Ruocco V. Clin Dermatol. 2013 Jul–Aug; 31(4):467-47.

Metals in cosmetics: implications for human health. Borowska S., Brzóska M.M.
J Appl Toxicol. 2015 Jun; 35(6):551-72.

Nickel sulphate allergy

Nickel is easily found and is a universal substance. It is contained in almost all metal alloys and is used in numerous consumer products such as detergents, cosmetics, dyes, fixers, stains, and more. Unlike other contact dermatitis, that of nickel is more widespread. Nickel dermatite has no specific site and may not be located.

The allergic reaction is delayed. In fact, it occurs about 24 to 36 hours after contact. This is a common situation. A woman puts on silver earrings and, after a day she finds herself with the red, edematous, itchy lobes. A similar reaction could also occur after she touches the button on her pants or the metal hook of her bra.

The allergic reaction tends to calm down after contact with nickel ceases, until the symptoms disappear. New contact, even in locations other than that previously exposed, can cause the appearance of similar skin reactions.

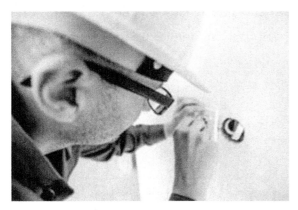 

It is very important to try to avoid contact with nickel. Although this may be possible for many people, it may be more difficult for those whose profession exposes them to nickel. For these people it is advisable to use protective equipment such as gloves or protective creams which limit direct and prolonged contact with the allergen in question.

As previously mentioned, nickel can cause allergies even when consumed orally. Ingesting nickel-rich foods can cause similar reactions to that of contact dermatitis, an eczematous, itchy, reaction on the skin.

To limit allergic reactions, it is essential to follow a low nickel diet. The total amount of allergen consumed during the day is the main factor to consider. Therefore, when planning a diet, the person suffering from the nickel allergy should track total daily intake, limiting the intake of products with high nickel content.

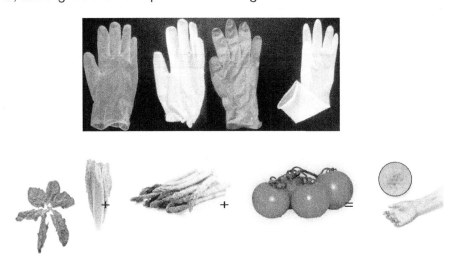

In this book you will find a quick guide to foods that are richer in nickel, and therefore should not be consumed. You will also find information about foods that have little or no nickel and can be consumed freely.

Systemic contact dermatitis to foods: nickel, BOP, and more. Fabbro S.K., Zirwas M.J.
Curr Allergy Asthma Rep. 2014 Oct; 14(10):463.

Diet and dermatitis: food triggers. Katta R., Schlichte M.
J Clin Aesthet Dermatol. 2014 Mar; 7(3):30-6.

Prevalence of nickel allergy in Europe following the EU Nickel Directive–a review. Ahlström M.G., Thyssen J.P., Menné T., Johansen J.D.
Contact Dermatitis. 2017 Oct; 77(4):193-200.

The SNAS

SNAS (systemic nickel allergy syndrome) is a syndrome characterized by a dietary intolerance to nickel. Symptoms affect the gastrointestinal tract and can include as swelling, diarrhea and cramps, frequently accompanied by eczema and itchy skin.

The diagnosis of SNAS is based anamnesis and patch tests. A negative result of the epicutaneous nickel sulphate test fully confirms that the patient does not have SNAS. On the other hand, a positive result does not confirm a SNAS diagnosis. Many sulphate allergy sufferers who react to nickel either through contact or ingestion show symptoms only through the skin, usually through widespread very itchy eczema that is resistant to therapy.

The percentage of people with nickel allergies varies by region. In Europe studies confirm that percentage of the population with nickel allergies varies from 8 to 18% with a female prevalence of 4 to 1. About 40% of these patients show reactions also on the gastrointestinal tract.

Now we can begin to understand the pathogenesis of SNAS. We know that the nickel contact dermatitis is based on a type IV immune response according to the classification of Gell and Coombs (therefore a cellular response mediated by lymphocytes, and not humoral, ie mediated by IgE).

Gell & Coombs Classification	
Type I	Anaphylaxis
Type II	Cytotoxic
Type III	Immune complex disease
Type IV	Delayed
Type V	stimulatory
Type VI	Killer cells
Type VII	Antibodyi anti–receptor

There is no information available about the pathology of the intestinal tract. The most probable hypothesis, still an educated guess, is that the same mechanism that leads to inflammation of the dermis can affect the mucous membrane of the gastrointestinal tract leading to local inflammation and consequent visceral symptoms.

Here are the most common symptoms:

- meteorism
- • flatulence
- • cramps
- • heartburn
- • gas colic
- • diarrhea
-

- • general malaise
- • nausea
- • headache
- • widespread itching
- • abdominal swelling
- • obesity

SNAS therapy is based entirely on a low-nickel diet. In literature there are many diets that focus on reducing the content of nuts. It is difficult to understand what led well-known doctors to different conclusions. Perhaps, as mentioned above, different locations have plants with different levels of nickel. Another possibility is that studies have been completed during different periods of the year. What is certain is that the most important consideration is what the patient reports: the effects of a food on a person is key in creating a successful diet with low nickel content.

Systemic contact dermatitis. Veien N.K.
Int J Dermatol. 2011 Dec; 50(12):1445-56.

Contact dermatitis as a systemic disease. Kulberg A., Schliemann S., Elsner P.
Clin Dermatol. 2014 May–Jun; 32(3):414-9. doi: 10.1016/j.clindermatol.2013.11.008.

Systemic contact dermatitis.
Nijhawan R.I., Molenda M., Zirwas M.J., Jacob S.E. Dermatol Clin. 2009 Jul; 27(3):355-64.

Irritable Bowel Syndrome and Nickel Allergy: What Is the Role of the Low Nickel Diet?
Rizzi A., Nucera E., Laterza L., Gaetani E., Valenza V., Corbo G.M., Inchingolo R., Buonomo A., Schiavino D., Gasbarrini A.
J Neurogastroenterol Motil. 2017 Jan 30; 23(1):101-108.

A low nickel diet

Food with high nickel content according to different sources

	A	B	C	D	E	F	G	H	I	L	M
almonds	■				■		■		■		■
apricots					■						
Asparagus			■								
Avocado											
Baking powder		■	■			■					■
beans	■	■	■	■			■	■			■
Beer					■						
Broccoli					■						
Cabbage			■								■
Carrots					■				■		
Cashevnuts									■		
Caulifower					■	■					■
Cocoa chocolade	■	■	■	■	■						
Cocunut power									■		■
Coffee											■
Corn			■		■						
Crustaceans						■					
Dried fruits		■				■					
Figs					■						■
Garlic											
Hazelnuts		■	■		■	■	■	■	■		
herring		■		■							■
Lentils	■										■
Lettuce			■								
Licorice		■			■	■					
Linseed								■			
Mackerel						■					
Margarine			■		■						■
Mushrooms			■	■	■						

	A	B	C	D	E	F	G	H	I	L	M
nuts	■			■	■	■	■	■	■	■	■
porrige	■	■		■	■	■	■	■	■		■
Onion			■	■			■	■	■	■	■
Peanuts	■	■		■	■	■	■				■
Pears		■		■		■	■				■
Peas	■	■		■	■		■	■			■
Pistachio							■		■		■
Poppy seeds							■				■
Potato					■						■
Prunes											■
Raisin			■								■
Raspberries											■
Rhubarb			■		■						■
Rie		■			■	■					■
Salmon									■		■
Shellfish						■	■	■			■
Soybean seeds		■	■		■	■	■	■			■
Spinach	■		■								■
Sunflower seeds			■								■
Tap water (initial flow)											■
tea		■		■	■						■
tomatoes			■			■					■
Tuna					■		■				■
Whole wheat flour		■		■	■		■				■

a) Flynholm 1984 [1], b) Veien [2, 3]; c) 1994 Venuti [4] d) Christensen 1999; e) Schiavino et al. 2006 [5] f) Sharma 2007 [5], g) Falagiani, Schiavino et al. 2008 [8] h) Veien, 1993 [8], i) Swedish Food Administration [28], l) Fonacier 2010 [7]; m) Picarelli 2010 [30

a). Flyvholm MA, Nielsen GD, Andersen A. Nickel content of food and estimation of dietary intake. Z Lebensm Unters Forsch. 1984; 179 (6):427-31

b). Veien NK, Hattel T, Justesen O, Norholm A. Dietary treatment of nickel dermatitis. Acta Derm Venereol Suppl (Stockh). 1985; 65:138-42.

c). Venuti A, Di Fonso M, Romano A. Allergia al nichel: stato dell'arte. Not Allerg 1994; 13:95-7.

d) 6. Schiavino D, Nucera E, Alonzi C, et al. A clinical trial of oral hyposensitization in systemic allergy to nickel. Int J Immunopathol Pharmacol 2006; 19(3):593-600

e. Schiavino D, Nucera E, Alonzi C, et al. A clinical trial of oral hyposensitization in systemic allergy to nickel. Int J Immunopathol Pharmacol 2006; 19(3):593-600. 27.

f. Sharma AD. Relationship between nickel allergy and diet. Indian J Dermatol Venereol Leprol 2007; 73:307-12.

g) Falagiani P, Di Gioacchino M, Ricciardi L, et al. Systemic nickel allergy syndrome (SNAS). A review. Rev Port Imunoalergologia 2008; 16 (2):135-47.

h) Veien NK, Hattel T, Laurberg G. Low nickel diet: an open, prospective trial. J Am Acad Dermatol. 1993; 29:1002-7.

i) . www.melisa.org/nickel.php (site web)

l) . Fonacier L, Dreskin S, Leung D. Allergic Skin Disease. J Allergy Clin. Immunol 2010; 125:S138-49.

m) Picarelli A, Di Tola M, Vallecoccia A, et al. Oral mucosa patch test: a new tool to recognize and study the adverse effects of dietary nickel exposure. Biol Trace Elem Res 2010 Mar 5 (Epub ahead of print)

A typical European diet contains 300-600 micrograms of nickel per day, mainly coming from vegetables. Some factors influence the intake of nickel in a diet. For example, eating oranges, foods rich in high vitamin C, and milk can all greatly reduce the intake of nickel. Anemia, on the other hand, is a condition that increases the body's absorption of nickel. Therefore, treating anemia through martial therapy can reduce the absorption of nickel. Moreover, two of the exact same types of vegetables can contain different levels of nickel since the concentration of nickel is influenced by where the plant is grown, the season, and even the age of the plant's leaves.

To achieve a low nickel diet, it is important not to eat many foods with high nickel content in one day. While the food allergies that cause urticaria are not dependent on the dose (a gram of peanuts or a pound makes no difference), as far as nickel is concerned, the manifestation of the allergy is strictly connected to the quantity assumed.

Low nickel diet in dermatology. Sharma A.D.
Indian J Dermatol. 2013 May; 58(3):24.

Relationship between nickel allergy and diet. Sharma A.D.
Indian J Dermatol Venereol Leprol. 2007 Sep–Oct; 73(5):307–12.

Nickel content of food and estimation of dietary intake. Flyvholm M.A., Nielsen G.D., Andersen A.
Z Lebensm Unters Forsch. 1984 Dec; 179(6): 427–31.

What Role Does Diet Play in the Management of Nickel Allergy? Cunningham E.
J Acad Nutr Diet. 2017 Mar; 117(3):500.

Diet and dermatitis: food triggers. Katta R.., Schlichte M.
J Clin Aesthet Dermatol. 2014 Mar; 7(3):30-6.

The table below lists the nickel content in some foods and was originally reported in a paper by Rizzi et al (2017). This should be kept in mind when following a low nickel diet.

Ni 100 µg/kg	Ni 200 µg/kg	Ni 500 µg/kg	Ni >500 µg/kg
Carrots	Apricot	Artichokes	Almonds
Figs	Broccoli	Asparagus	Chickpeas
Lettuce	Corn	Beans	Cacao
Green salad	Lobster and crab	Cabbag	Tomato Concentrate
Liquorice	Onions	Cauliflower	Lentils
Mushrooms	Pears	Green beans	Wheat
Plaice (fish)	Raisins	Whole wheat products	Nuts
Cod		Yeast	Peanuts
Rhubarb		Margarine	
Tea		Mussels	
		Oysters	
		Potatoes	
		Peas	
		Plums	
		Spinach	
		Tomatoes	

Risks of a nickel-free diet

As we have seen nickel is contained in many vegetables. Therefore, a person with a nickel allergy is forced to follow a dict containing very few vegetables.

We know that an adequate intake of vegetables and fruit is an essential component in a healthy, balanced diet since these foods are rich in fiber, vitamins, minerals, and more. Let's take a deeper look at the benefits of vegetables and fruit consumption in the diet.

Fruits and vegetables are rich in fiber. This fiber, once in the intestine, delays the absorption of sugar and prevents peaks of hyperglycemia. Hyperglycemia can be harmful for the glycemic metabolism because it can induce the release of insulin which in turn, over time, causes a metabolic syndrome resulting in obesity. No less important is the function of fiber in the regulation of the cinesis and of the intestinal transit. Fiber is made up mostly of cellulose, a substance that is not digested by our intestines and is excreted thus creating fecal mass and facilitating defecation.

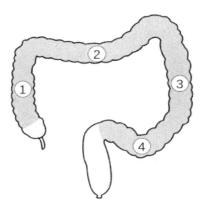

Blue/purple		Eggplant Blueberries Plums	AnthocyaninPot assium Magnesium
White		Onions Garlic porri	Plyphenols Selenium Potatssiu m
Green		Asparagus Broccoli Spinach	Folic acid Beta carotene Lutein
Yellow		Lemos Grapegruit Carrots	Vitamin C Potassium Flavanoids
Red		Tomatoes Strawberri es Peppers	AnthocyaninLyc opene Selenium

Finally, fiber helps one to feel full and therefore, helps us to limit the intake of other foods, counteracting obesity. The WHO recommends eating 25 grams of fiber per day which would mean 350 to 450 grams of fruit and/or

vegetables. The WHO recommends to always consume fruits and vegetables of different colors. This is important since different colors correspond to different substances. The body needs various substances, and therefore, you cannot only eat oranges and mandarins enriched with vitamin C and neglect all other vitamins.

Furthermore, vegetables help support colon health (see Mediterranean diet) which is linked to the prevention of colon cancer. Carotenoids, selenium, zinc, and flavonoids are all found often in vegetables. These substances have an important antioxidant function, neutralizing free radicals that are harmful to the body and preventing the build-up of cholesterol on the artery walls.

Potassium and magnesium are also commonly found in vegetables and are incredibly important for our metabolism. Potassium is the element that causes both the contraction of muscle fibrocells and synaptic transmission between nerve cells.

Factors that influence nickel absorption

There are some factors that influence the absorption of nickel in a diet:

1. anemia;
2. smoking;
3. cooking methods.

Anemia is the deficiency of hemoglobin in the blood. Hemoglobin is a protein that binds to oxygen and transports it from the lungs to tissues throughout the body. Then, it is used in the Krebs cycle to supply energy to our body. Anemia, in addition to causing a sense of tiredness, alopecia, and mood changes, also encourages the absorption of nickel. Therefore, it is of even more importance for a nickel-allergic patient is to correct the values of hemoglobin. Once the blood levels of sideremia, folic acid and vitamin B12 are in order, the patient must take iron, folate, and vitamin B12 orally to restore hemoglobin values.

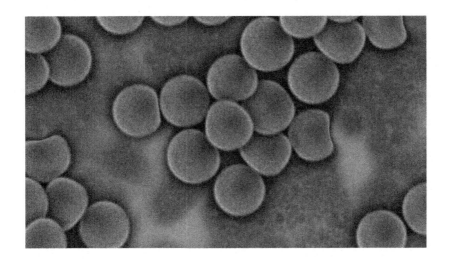

It is common knowledge that smoking causes lung and bladder cancer, damages the lungs, leads to chronic bronchitis, and causes pulmonary emphysema. Smoking can also increase the risk of infarction, tissues death, and atherosclerosis, the buildup of fats, chloesterol, and other substances in the artery walls which can restrict blood flow.

Maybe less commonly known, smoking also promotes the absorption of nickel. In fact, the combustion of tobacco creates a substance called "nickel-carbonyl" which is inhaled by the smoker. This substance reaches the pulmonary alveoli and is absorbed by the blood where it favors the haemoconcentration of nickel.

Cooking food can decrease the nickel concentration in food. It is essential that the food is cooked in nickel-free pans made of non-ferrous materials such as teflon, ceramic, or glass. If you are using steel pans check that they are in 18/10 stainless steel. When cooking food in an oven, cooking sheets must be covered with baking paper. As for stiring, one should choose a spoon made of wood or polycarbonate material, especially at high temperatures.

Gastrointestinal absorption of metals.
Diamond G.L., Goodrum P.E., Felter S.P., Ruoff W.L. Drug Chem Toxicol. 1998 May; 21(2):223-51.

The epicutaneous test, also called the patch test

The patch test is a special test used to diagnose cutaneous and diffusive allergic skin reactions. The causes of these types of dermatitis can be traced back to the contact with or ingestion of chemical substances often contained in commonly used objects or foods. The mechanism of contact allergy is cellular or delayed type IV in the classification of allergic reactions according to Gell and Coombs.

The reaction to the allergen is therefore of cellular type and not of antibodies, and, as the name says, is not immediate but delayed. When a patient has contact with an allergen the allergic reaction occurs after about 12 to 24 hours after, unlike the classic humoral or immediate allergy that occurs within a few minutes of contact.

Here's how the test is performed:

The patient comes to the office, having been sure not to take cortisone and/or antihistamines for a week. On a special patch the doctor deposits chemicals (allergens) and the patch is applied to the patient's back.

The patient should refrain from sports and should not bath or shower until the patch is removed by the doctor after 48 to 72 hours. The evaluation will be performed when the patch is removed. Some substances will not cause a reaction. However, in case of a positive correspondence of the chemical substance with an allergy, a local allergic reaction will be present through redness, appearance of eczema, and intense itching. This reaction will clear up on its own within 2 or 3 days

.

The following is an example of a standard series that is commonly used for allergy evaluation:

SolfaNikel sulfate

Paraphenylenediamine

Mercaptobenzothiazole

Tetramethylthiuramdisulfid

Balsam of Peru

Formalin

Turpentine

Sodium bisulfite Benzocaine

Perfumes mix

Phenylcyclohexylparaphen

Ylenediamine

Difenilparaendiamina

Lattice

Clorochinaldolo

Colofonia

Acido benzoico

Lanolina

Bicromato di potassio

Cloruro di cobalto

Disperso giallo

Disperso rosso

Disperso blu

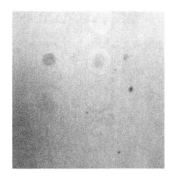 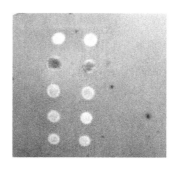

The correlation between celiac disease and nickel allergies

Many professionals have noticied a correlation between celiac disease and nickel allergies. To understand how the two phenomena can be associated, it is necessary to consider the pathogenesis of celiac disease, autoimmune pathology, and the fundamental role of the intestinal barrier.

Celiac disease is a systemic autoimmune disease that can affect all organs and systems. The cornerstone of the pathogenesis is the production of autoantibodies (anti-transglutaminases and anti-endomysium) that activate gastrointestinal immune response. This then leads the destruction of the mucous membrane (villous atrophy) in genetically predisposed subjects (presence of HLA alleles DQ2 and / or DQ8).

Exposure to gluten triggers autoimmune response. Currently, other environmental factors that determine the development of the disease are unknown. Gluten, contained especially in wheat, barley, rye, spelt, and many other cereals are composed of two proteins: gliadin and glutenin. In genetically predisposed subjects, ingested gliadin is activated by an enzyme (tissue transglutaminase). This transformation then activates the T lymphocytes, which regulates the production of numerous pro-inflammatory cytokines including interleukin-2, interleukin-4, interferon gamma, TNF (tumor necrosis factor) alpha. The consumption of these toxic substances causes damage characterized by the flattening of intestinal villi and hyperplasia of intestinal crypts.

 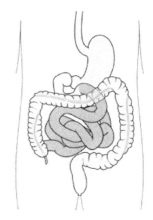

The intestinal barrier is a structure that acts as a filter and prevents the absorption of large molecules, such as proteins, in the intestine. The barrier is also able to recognize the difference between "self" and "non-self" molecules. This is thanks to the presence of "localized" antibodies between the intestinal cells which allows the recognition of viruses and bacteria, preventing their internalization.

This mechanism allows the body to block the movement of pathogens. Likewise, even macromolecules, such as proteins with high molecular weights, cannot pass through the barrier and remain in the intestinal lumen.

Therefore, it can be concluded that in the absence of the intestinal barrier the mucous membrane would absorb all proteins consumed in a diet. This would lead to serious changes of the individual's homeostasis.

Now, let's dive into why the celiac subject is more likely to suffer from nickel allergies. This can happen for two reason. First, celiac disease, as we have seen, creates damage to the mucous membrane of the intestinal wall in conditions of complete restitutio ad integrum failure. This can cause an altered passage of substances through the same lesions in the intestinal barrier.

Furthermore, the only treatment that has been found to be effective for celiac disease is a gluten-free diet which is when the celiac subject eats foods that naturally contain larger quantities of nuts, such as corn and vegetables.

Contact reactions to foods

Contact dermatitis (DAC), widely discussed in another chapter of this book, can manifest itself through contact with the "oleoresins" present in some vegetables and fruits. The main allergen is the "sequiretene", which can be found in high quantities in many vegetables (broccoli, turnips, cabbage) and in some fruits (lemons, oranges) (1), (2), (3).

Irritative contact dermatitis (DIC) is an acute dermatitis that occurs when a person encounters certain foods and is not immune mediated. Instead, it is the result of a simple irritation and, unlike the DAC, it is not delayed but instead, is immediate. A histological examination of the lesions does not show the presence of cells typical to the immune allergic reaction. The substances that most commonly cause inactive dermatitis are lemons, garlic, pineapples, radishes.

Allergic urticaria is an immediate immunological reaction that is characterized by the involvement of IgE. Therefore, it can affect potentially allergic subjects. The allergic patient is sensitive to specific foods and to the subsequent contact when an allergic reaction occurs. This is usually characterized by intense itching and the appearance of wheals (4), (5), (6).

Non-allergic contact urticaria is like DIC but is distinguished by the appearance of the lesions. This reaction, unlike that of DIC, is characterized by numerous wheals and the involvement of chemical inflammation mediators, such as histamine and citochiine. (7), (8).

Systemic contact dermatitis to foods: nickel, BOP, and more. Fabbro S.K., Zirwas M.J.
Curr Allergy Asthma Rep. 2014 Oct; 14(10):463.

Cutaneous Manifestation of Food Allergy. Tam J.S.
Immunol Allergy Clin North Am. 2017 Feb; 37(1):217–231.

Contact allergy to food. Brancaccio RR, Alvarez MS. Dermatol Ther. 2004; 17(4):302–13.

When should the diagnosis 'contact urticaria' be used? Aalto-Korte K.
Contact Dermatitis. 2017 Nov; 77(5):323-324. doi: 10.1111/cod.12884. Epub 2017 Sep 21.

A Case of Anaphylaxis Induced by Contact with Young Radish (Raphanus sativus L). Lee Y.H., Lee J.H., Kang H.R., Ha J.H., Lee B.H., Kim S.H.

Allergy Asthma Immunol Res. 2015 Jan; 7(1):95–7. Immunologic contact urticaria.
McFadden J.
Immunol Allergy Clin North Am. 2014 Feb; 34(1):157-67.

Contact reactions to food. Killig C., Werfel T.
Curr Allergy Asthma Rep. 2008 May ;8(3):209–14.

Garlic (Allium sativum L.): adverse effects and drug interactions in humans. Borrelli F,. Capasso R., Izzo A.A.
Mol Nutr Food Res. 2007 Nov; 51(11):1386-97.
Occupational contact urticaria and protein contact dermatitis. Doutre M.S.
Eur J Dermatol. 2005 Nov–Dec; 15(6):419–24.

Food intolerances: fake news or reality?

We often see deceptive advertising on television that has the power to influence our decision making. I wonder why there is not a government organization that censors "scam" advertising. The issue becomes even more serious when this type of marketing influences our health. In Italy, each year three hundred million euros is spent on useless "pseudo"-studies that focus on discovering non-existent food intolerances.

Let's take stock of the situation. First we need to distinguish the difference between allergic reactions and food intolerances. Allergic reactions are those reactions mediated by IgE-type antibodies that are not dose-dependent, manifest with skin rashes, itching, edemas, and begin immediately after taking the substance (10-30minutes). These reactions affect genetically predisposed individuals and can be studied with appropriate scientific analyses.

Food intolerances have been defined as "non-allergic allergies" (Kaplan 1991), reactions in the organism not mediated by IgE. Two, and only two types, are scientifically proven, lactose and gluten intolerances.

There are numerous tests on the market that can uncover all intolerances the patient has. These tests, however, have never been tested on a valid sample size of people to ascertain their validity. To be considered reliable, a test must include two essential elements: sensitivity and specificity.

Let's try to understand the meaning of these two terms. A test has valid sensitivity when it can identify all patients who are clinically ill. This means that 100% of sick subjects must show positive results when given the test. Therefore, the patient who tests negative is certainly a negative patient also from the clinical point of view.

The specificity of a test concerns the percentage of patients who, certainly from the clinical perspective, show positive results but are actually false positives. The higher the number of false positivite results, the less reliable the test.

To understand with even more depth, here are some practical examples:

1. Anna is a patient with celiac disease: she carries out a test for this disease and it is positive, therefore nothing to add is perfect.

2. Loredana, who is not suffering from celiac disease, carries out a test that is positive. Here is the specificity above, it is a false positive.

3. Roberta, of whom we have no medical history, carries out a test for celiac disease which is negative. For what has been said before regarding sensitivity, we are sure that she is not affected by celiac disease.

In summary, for a test to be reliable it must have a sensitivity of 100% and sufficient specificity.

Therefore, before wasting time and money, it would be best if scientific experts were transparent about the reliability of tests for food intolerances. Such tests are continually proposed by various laboratories and sometimes, even more seriously, even by "doctors".

Clinical cases

Case number one

A 38 year-old patient has come to an appointment complaining about the presence of dermatitis on both hands for about a year. There are no noteworthy diseases in the patient's medical history. In the physiologic anamnesis the patient reports that she gave birth to her first child about one year ago. Patches are applied to conduct a patch test. After 48 hours patch tests are read and show a clear positive result for nickel sulphate.

This positive result aligns with the patient's medical history as she reports using detergents and soaps for cleaning over the past year in a vastly different way than before she had a baby. It should also be considered that hormonal variations, such as those that occur during and after pregnancy, can trigger a latent allergy.

Case number two

Marco is a 16-year-old student who has scheduled a visit due to the appearance of dermatitis on the fingertips of his left hand. He is not left-handed. There is nothing significant in the physiologic and pathologic history and no appearance of lesions on the rest of the body. Patch tests are completed and show strong positivity to nickel sulphate. The results of the patch test does not explain why it is only on the left hand.

However, an accurate re-examination of the physiologic anamnesis, in the light of what we have found, allows us to discover that the boy spends more time playing guitar than studying. That is the reason why dermatitis is only in the left hand.

Case number three

A patient suffering from a nickel allergy, established a few years earlier by patch testing, comes to the office. Today, the patient is suffering from heartburn and intestinal cramps accompanied by coughing. The patient believes that nickel is responsible for gastrointestinal symptoms which requires an adequate diet and/or therapy. A careful analysis of the patient's medical history allows us to identify that the symptoms are more severe during the night and when fasting and not when consuming foods containing nickel. Nevertheless, we ask the patient to follow a nickel-free diet for 15 days. At the end of the diet the patient noted no improvement and, therefore, an antiacid is administered and a new diet is recommended to the patient to help with acid reflux.

After fifteen days the patient returns and reports a significant improvement in symptoms. A subsequent gastroscopy confirms the presence of gastritis with hiatal hernia and reflux. This time the famous culprit, nickel, is innocent!

Case number four

A gastroenterologist orders a test for a patient with suspected food intolerance. The patient reports abdominal swelling and flatulence after eating foods with a high nickel content. In the pathologic anamnesis there are no signs suggesting nickel-related dermatitis. A patch test is administered and shows positivity to nickel sulphate. The conclusion is a diagnosis of SNAS not associated with DAC.

Clinical case number 5

One of our patients suffering from nickel-based dermatitis comes to the office showing sudden skin aggravation, particularly in the limbs without any known reason. The patient's physiologic history is carefully studied, but nothing suspicious emerges. After various types of therapy, with almost no results, a biopsy is ordered. The outcome of the biopsy suggests psoriasis dermatitis, but the similar appearance of lesions confuses dermatologists and allergists, suggesting an exacerbation of contact dermatitis.

.

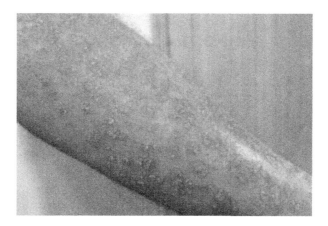

The oral hypo-sensitizing treatment for nickel allergies

Reactions to this metal, present in many objects and even foods, can be stopped with nickel hypo-sensitizing treatment (TIO NICHEL). For the more severe forms of nickel allergies, defined as systemic, an oral nickel hypo-sensitizing treatment has been successfully tested. This is not a traditional prophylaxis but, within eight to ten months, this treatment has been proven to show significant improvement in seven out of ten patients' symptoms. Diarrhea and stomachaches are common symptoms. Of the approximately nine million Italians allergic to this metal, almost two develop the systemic form. But what does systemic mean? It means that in addition to classic contact dermatitis, caused by an infinite number of nickel-containing objects (from coins to jewels, from cell phones to cosmetics), the symptom body also reacts to oral consumption of nickel. This can cause pain, hives and eczema on the abdominal area, diarrhea, stomach swelling, bloating, vomiting, and gastroesophageal reflux. And, even in this case, avoiding metal is not easy as it is found in many fruits and vegetables and water. It can even be absorbed by eating a plate of pasta that was cooked in stainless steel pot. The oral nickel hypo-sensitizing treatment is prescribed only at the end of a complete diagnostic procedure, which starts with a patch test. In this test, a disk containing nickel sulphate is applied with a bandage to the skin and left in place for 48-72 hours. If, at the end of the examination, dermatitis is detected in the contact area, we proceed with six to eight weeks of a low nickel diet. Once the diagnosis is confirmed, oral therapy can begin which involves taking 500 nanograms of nickel (half a millionth of a gram) three times a week for six months. Therefore, in the following three months, foods containing nickel are gradually reintroduced and finally a free regime is reintroduced.

The epidemiology of contact allergy in the general population – prevalence and main findings. Thyssen J.P., Linneberg A., Menné T., Johansen J.D.
Contact Dermatitis 2007; 57: 287-99.

Systemic nickel allergy syndrome: nosologic framework and diet regimen.
Braga M., Quecchia C., Perotta C., Timpini A., Maccarinelli K., Di Tommaso L., Di Gioacchino M. Int J Immunopthol Pharmacol 2013; 26: 707–16.

Oral hyposensitization to nickel allergy: preliminary clinical results.
Panzani R.C., Schiavino D., Nucera E., Pellegrino S., Fais G., Schinco G., Patriarca G. Int Arch Allergy Immunol 1995; 107: 251-4.

Expression of lymphocyte subpopulations, cytokine serum levels and blood and urine trace elements in nickel sensitized women.
Boscolo P., Di Gioacchino M., Conti P., Barbacane R.C., Andreassi M., Di Giacomo F., Sabbioni E. Life Sci 1998; 63: 1417-22.

Systemic effects of ingested nickel on the immune system of nickel sensitized women. Boscolo P., Andreassi M., Sabbioni E., Reale M., Conti P., Amerio P., Di Gioacchino M. Life Sci. 1999; 64: 1485-91.

Systemic contact dermatitis after oral exposure to nickel: a review with a modified meta–analysis. Jensen C.S., Menné T., Johansen J.D.
Contact Dermatitis 2006; 54: 79-86.
Systemic nickel allergy syndrome. Schiavino D.
Int J Immunopathol Pharmacol 2005; 18: 7-10.

Nickel systemic contact dermatitis.
Verna N., Di Claudio F., Balatsinou L., Schiavone C., Caruso R., Renzetti A., Gabriele E., Turi M.C., Feliziani A., Di Gioacchino M.
Int J Immunopathol Pharmacol 2005; 18: 11-4.

Serum levels of sICAM-1 in subjects affected by systemic nickel allergy syndrome. Minciullo P.L., Saija D., Trombetta D., Ricciardi L., Di Pasquale G., Gangemi S.
It J Allergy Clin Immunol 2006; 16: 109-13.

Appetizers

Buttered anchovies

Ingredients:

8 anchovies

Butter- to taste

Preparation:

Start with eight anchovies in oil. Clean the fish off the bones and arrange them on a plate, layering them. For the next step, the butter must be very cold from the refrigerator and a butter curler must be very cold and wet with cold water. Use the curler on the butter to create eight curls to be placed on the anchovies and accompanied with slices of homemade bread.

Bruschetta

Ingredients:

♣ 4 slices of homemade bread

♣ 4 tablespoons of extra virgin olive oil

salt and pepper

Preparation:

Toast four slices of homemade bread without burning them. Top them with oil. Sprinkle them with salt and pepper. Be sure to eat them while they are still warm either on their own or as an accompaniment to raw ham.

Salmon carpaccio

Ingredients:

* 150 grams of salmon
* 1 small piece of butter
* 1 lemon
* 1 orange
* 1 small piece of fennel
* A dash of pink pepper

Preparation:

Take 150 grams of raw swordfish cut very thinly. Arrange it carefully on a plate greased with butter. Pour the lemon juice over and add some butter curls. Cut the orange and fennel into thin slices and add this and a dash of green pepper atop the swordfish. Place the dish in the refrigerator for half an hour and serve.

Shrimp cocktail

✗✗✗

◔◔

💰💰💰💰

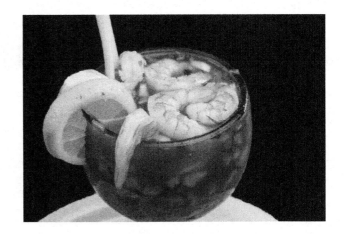

Ingredients:

* 2 ounces of shrimp
* 50 grams of mayonnaise
* 1 lemon

Preparation:

Buy 200 grams of fresh shrimp. Blanch them by bringing a large pot of water to a rolling boil. Add the shrimp and cook for a few minutes. When the shrimp turn pink, remove them, and submerge them in cold water. Dry the shrimp and clean them with a sharp knife. Be sure to wash the meaty part well, dry them, and put them in a bowl. Now add some mayonnaise and a few slices of lemon to garnish. Refrigerate for half an hour and serve.

Sea bass bruschetta

✗✗

🕐

💰 💰 💰

Ingredients:

- ♣ 1 fillet of sea bass
- ♣ 4 slices of homemade bread
- ♣ 4 tablespoons of extra virgin olive oil
- ♣ Salt and pepper

Preparation:

Toast four slices of homemade bread without burning them and set aside.
Put the sea bass fillet in a saucepan, add oil and salt, and fry over low heat.
While it cooks use a wooden spoon to try to break it into tiny pieces. When
you see that the fillet is browned, taste it to check. When it is ready, add salt.
At this point, with the help of a spatula, coat the slices of bread well and
serve.

Cream frites

⚒⚒⚒

🕐🕐🕐

💰💰

Ingredients:

- ♣ 2 eggs
- ♣ 1 hectogram of flour
- ♣ 2 tablespoons of sugar
- ♣ 1 lemon
- ♣ Half a glass of milk

Preparation:

Beat two egg yolks in a bowl with the sugar and flour. Add the grated lemon peel and cook over low heat until you see that the mixture seperates on its own from the pan. Take it off the heat, place it on baking paper and let it cool. When it's cold, cut the mixture into small rhombuses. Dip each into beaten egg white, lightly flour, and place in boiling oil to fry. Sprinkle sugar on top and serve warm.

Seafood salad

�✗✗✗

🕐🕐🕐

💰💰💰

Ingredients: ♣ 4 ounces of clams ♣ 4 ounces of mussels ♣ 4 ounces of squid ♣ 4 ounces of octopus ♣ 1 clove of garlic ♣ Lemon, salt and oil

Preparation:

Carefully clean the octopus and rub the surface well to remove the thin film that covers it. Put it in a pot and cook for about thirty minutes. Dip the octopus in water to make sure the tentacles curl well. Drain the octopus and put the squid and shrimp in the same cooking water and cook for about ten minutes. Drain them and put the clean mussels and clams in a pan. Cover with a lid, turn the heat up, and once they open, drain them. Let them cool. Cut the octopus and squid into strips and shell the mussels and clams. Season all with oil, salt and lemon and refrigerate before serving.

Sea bass paté

Ingredients:

- ♣ 1 fillet of sea bass
- ♣ 1 tablespoon of white wine
- ♣ 1 hectogram of 00 flour
- ♣ 100 grams of milk
- ♣ 20 grams of butter
- ♣ salt pepper

Preparation:

Put the sea bass fillet in a pyrex dish, add the butter and brown. At the same time, stir and crush the fillet. Pour in a drop of wine to help with cooking. As soon as you see that it is almost cooked add flour and milk. Cook for a few more minutes and then season with salt and pepper. Put everything in the blender and then chill. The dish should be served cold as an appetizer.

Codfish balls

✕✕✕

🕐🕐🕐🕐

💰 💰

Ingredients:

♣ 100 grams of cod

♣ 150 grams of potatoes

♣ 40 grams of butter

♣ 30 grams of cooked ham

♣ 30 grams of breadcrumbs

♣ 4 tablespoons of oil

♣ 3 tablespoons of milk

♣ 2 eggs

♣ 1 tablespoon of 00 flour

Preparation:

Boil the potatoes. Cut them into small pieces and put them in a bowl. Add butter and milk and use a wooden fork to mix everything together. Shred the cooked cod and cooked ham both shredded and, in another container, mix them with butter. Add everything together and mix. Then make small meatballs with your hands. Dip them in the beaten egg and then in breadcrumbs. Brown them in oil well being careful that the temperature is not too high. Serve on wax paper as a hot appetizer.

Ham and melon

Ingredients:

♣ Ham and melon

Preparation:

This is a remarkably simple summer appetizer. Cut the cantelope into small slices, possibly all the same size. Roll each piece in a slice of raw ham and secure everything with a toothpick. Put them in the fridge for an hour before serving.

Stuffed rusks

✕✕ ✕✕ ✕✕

🕐 🕐 🕐

💰 💰

Ingredients:

* 150 grams of puff pastry
* 50 grams of cheese
* 2 hot dogs
* 8 anchovies in oil

Preparation:

Use a glass to make a couple of dozen discs from the puff pastry dough.
Place them on baking paper and fill each disc with different ingredients,
some with cheese (as you like), others with pieces of sausage, and the rest
with anchovies. Pinch the outer edges with your hands and place in the oven.
When they are golden take them out of the oven and serve.

Sautéed clams

🛠🛠🛠🛠

🕐🕐🕐

💰💰💰

Ingredients:

- ♣ 800 grams of clams
- ♣ 4 tablespoons of oil
- ♣ 4 cloves of garlic
- ♣ Half a glass of white wine

Preparation:

Take a large pan and add four tablespoons of olive oil, a piece of chili pepper, and four cloves of garlic. Put it on low heat. After a few minutes, add a kilo and a half of well-cleaned clams into a pot with boiling water and cover with a lid. In a few minutes you will see that the clams will have opened. At this point pour in a half glass of white wine and cook a little longer with the lid half open. Once cooked, drain and sprinkle with parsley before serving.

Smoked kebabs

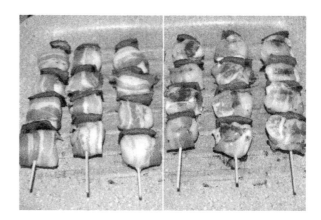

Ingredients:

♣ 1 hectogram of mini smoked scamorza balls

♣ 1 hectogram of proscuitto

Preparation:

This is an appetizer that you can serve either hot or cold. It is easy to prepare but this doesn't take away from its quality. Make sure you have eight wooden skewers. Wrap each of the smoked mozzarella balls in proscuitto and put four or five on each skewer. You can serve them cold or, if you prefer, you can put the in the oven for a few minutes to melt the cheese. Cooking will certainly make the dish heavier. In addition, you can also serve the kebabs on slices of toasted homemade bread.

Ground kebabs

Ingredients:

* ♣ 1 hectogram of mozzarella balls
* ♣ 1 hectogram of raw ham
* ♣ 50 grams of ciauscolo
* ♣ 4 cheese slices
* ♣ 4 hot dogs

Preparation:

If you have unexpected guests this is definitely the fastest and most substantial appetizer you can make. Take the ciauscolo and make small meatballs with your hands. Then cut the cheese slices into four parts. Now take a large wooden toothpick and insert the food alternately until the skewer is about half full. Place a slice of homemade bread on a plate and put the skewers on top.

first courses

Rice arancini

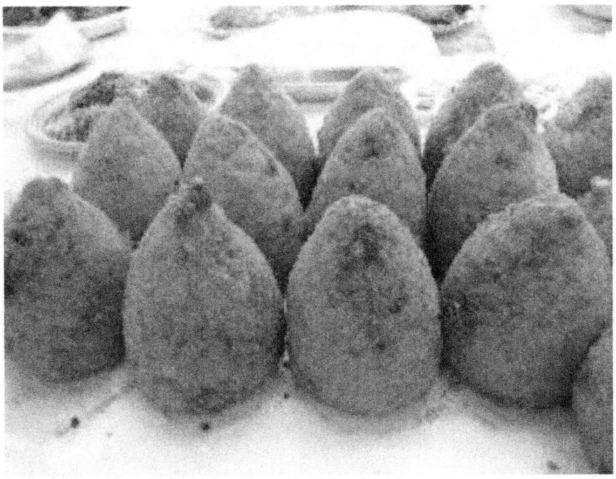

Ingredients:

- ♣ 150 grams of rice
- ♣ 30 grams of butter
- ♣ 1 egg
- ♣ 50 grams of parmesan cheese
- ♣ 125 grams of mozzarella
- ♣ 50 grams of ham

Preparation:

Boil 150 grams of rice in a little bit of water. When it is cooked add 30 grams of butter and a pinch of saffron. Take it off the heat and add a beaten egg and 50 grams of Parmesan cheese. Let it cool well and then use your hands to divide the mixture into four parts. Each of these parts should then be made into the shape of an "arancino". Next, create a hole inside of each and put in a piece of mozzarella and cooked ham. Close the ball of rice well and dip it in beaten egg and then breadcrumbs. Fry in plenty of oil and eat warm.

Neapolitan Calzone

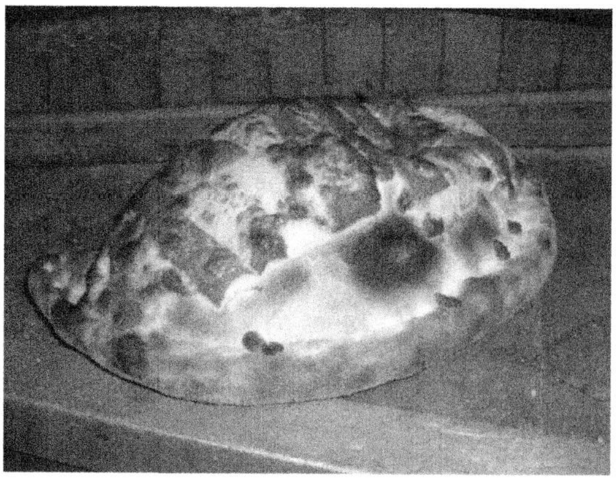

Ingredients:

- 200 grams of flour
- 7 grams of brewer's yeast
- 125 grams of mozzarella
- 100 grams of ham
- 1 egg
- oil to taste

Preparation:

Put the flour in a bowl and add the dissolved yeast a drop of water and a pinch of salt. Slowly, add half a glass of water and knead with your hands. Once kneaded, create a ball and put the dough aside Put the dough aside for 2 hours. After 2 hours, use the dough to create two pizzas of the thickness you prefer. Then add diced mozzarella, raw or cooked ham, and the beaten egg in the center. Close into a half-moon shape and seal the edges well with your hands. Put them in the oven at the maximum temperature for 10 minutes.

Cannelloni with ricotta and sausage

✕✕✕

🕐🕐🕐

💰💰💰

Ingredients:

* ♣ 6 cannelloni
* ♣ 2 sausages
* ♣ 300 grams of ricotta
* ♣ 1 egg
* ♣ 30 grams of butter
* ♣ 1 lemon
* ♣ 100 grams of bechamel
* ♣ 30 grams of Parmesan cheese

Preparation:

Mix the ricotta with the sausage, lemon zest, pepper, egg, and grated parmesan. Fill the cannelloni with the mixture and arrange them in a greased baking dish. Cover with the béchamel and sprinkle with grated parmesan cheese and flakes of butter. Put them in the oven and serve warm.

Fettuccine with meat sauce

⚒⚒⚒⚒

🕐🕐🕐🕐

💰💰💰💰

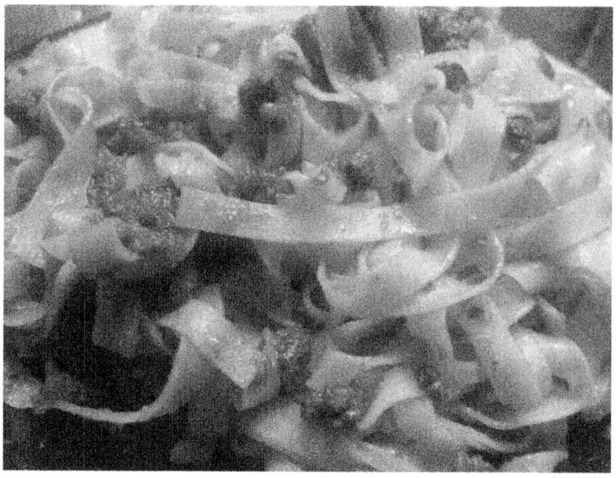

Ingredients:

- ♣ 3 ounces of ground beef
- ♣ 1 glass of red wine
- ♣ 30 grams of butter
- ♣ 1 carrot
- ♣ 1 piece of celery

Preparation:

Brown the chopped celery and carrots on low heat using two tablespoons of oil and a generous piece of butter. Next add the red wine and, when you see that the mixture becomes soft, add three ounces of minced beef. Then pour in a half glass of red wine and cover it. Cook on very low heat for three hours, adding red wine if necessary. When the sauce is finished add salt to your liking and pour over fettuccine (I recommend fresh pasta).

Gnocchi with gorgonzola

✗✗✗✗
🕐🕐🕐🕐
💰 💰

Ingredients:

- ♣ 1 half a kilo of potatoes
- ♣ flour
- ♣ 1 hectogram of gorgonzola
- ♣ 30 grams of Parmesan cheese
- ♣ 20 grams of butter

Preparation:

Boil the potatoes. Break them into small pieces with a fork. Then add and mix in flour using with your hands. Roll out the dough into long "snakes" which you will then cut with a knife to create individual gnocchi. Boil water and add salt. Once the water is boiling, add the gnocchi and, as soon as they come to the surface, remove the pan from the burner and drain. Season them with butter gorgonzola, and parmesan while they are still hot and serve.

Gricia pasta

✗✗✗✗

🕐🕐🕐

💰 💰

Ingredients:

- ♣ 1 hectogram of bacon
- ♣ 1 half a glass of white wine
- ♣ 2 ounces of pasta
- ♣ 50 grams of Parmesan cheese

Preparation:

Brown thinly sliced bacon over low heat using a tablespoon of olive oil and half a glass of white wine. Then add some black pepper and cover, leaving the lid open a bit to allow the alcohol to evaporate. If necessary, add more wine. When the bacon is done add cooked pasta and a heaping handful of parmesan cheese to the pan. Pour a few tablespoons of water from the pasta and stir with a wooden spoon to create a cream that covers the pasta.

Pasta with tuna

✗✗
🕐🕐
💰💰

Ingredients:

- ♣ 2 cloves of garlic
- ♣ 250 grams of tuna
- ♣ 2 ounces of pasta

Preparation:

Sautee two cloves of garlic without burning them and then add four anchovy fillets. Break the ancovies apart a wooden spatula while cooking. Next add 250 grams of drained tuna (in oil) and break it apart with the spoon. Cook for ten minutes over medium heat and remove the garlic. Add cooked pasta (al dente) to the pan, stir for a minute, and serve.

Ricotta soup

⚒⚒⚒⚒

🕐🕐🕐

💰💰

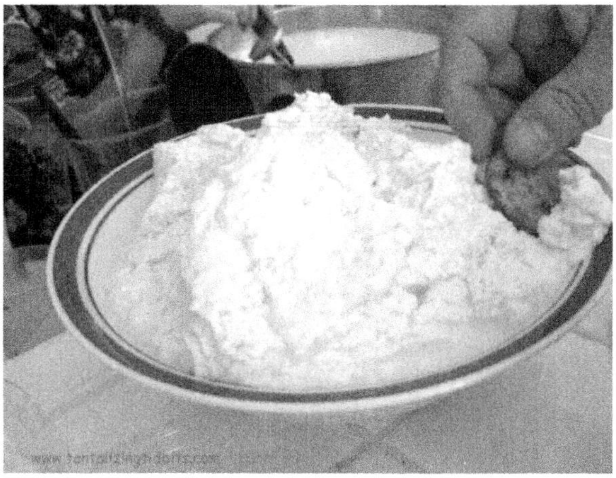

Ingredients:

- ♣ 2 ounces of ricotta
- ♣ 2 eggs
- ♣ 30 grams of parmesan cheese
- ♣ 1 half a liter of meat broth

Preparation:

Mix the ricotta with two eggs and add the parmesan cheese. Pour onto a plate, creating a layer about 1 centimeter high. Put it on top of a pot with boiling water, cover and cook in a “bain-marie”. When it has solidified, cut it into cubes, and pour it into the boiling broth.

Orecchiette with broccoli and sausage

Difficoltà ⚒⚒⚒⚒

Tempo 🕐🕐🕐

Costo 💰💰

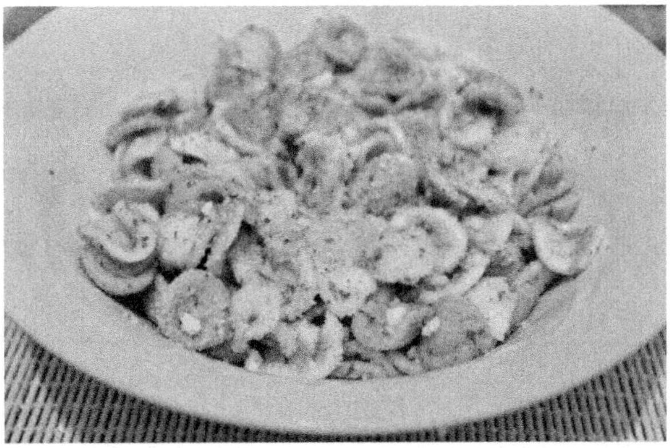

Ingredients:

- ♣ 2 ounces of pasta (orecchiette)
- ♣ 300 grams of broccoli
- ♣ 2 sausages
- ♣ 1 half a glass of white wine
- ♣ oil and black pepper

Preparation:

Broccoli has little nickel content and is therefore permitted in modest and occasional quantities. That said, this recipe calls for 300 grams of broccoli. Start by cleaning them well and leave them in the water. Now take two minced sausages, remove the skin and crumble them into a pan. Add a drizzel of oil and a drop of white wine and cook over low heat. When you see that the sausage starts to brown, add the broccoli (not fully drained) and continue cooking cooking on low heat. Cook the orecchiette pasta in boiling water and drain into the pan with broccoli and sausage. Cook and sprinkle with black pepper before serving.

Paccheri with calamari

Ingredients: ♣ 2 ounces of paccheri ♣ 3 ounces of squid ♣ 2 cloves of garlic ♣ 4 tablespoons of oil ♣ 1 glass of white wine

Preparation:

Cut a couple of squid into half centimeter rings. Heat four tablespoons of oil in a pan and add two cloves of garlic and a single pachino tomato (I recommend a small one). Then slowly add some white wine and cook on medium heat for 30 minutes. When the pasta is "al dente" drain and add to the pan to finish cooking.

Baked pasta

⚒⚒⚒

🕐🕐🕐

💰💰

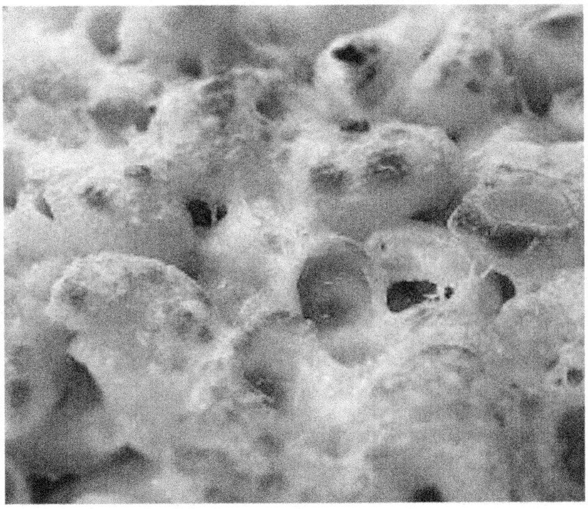

Ingredients:

♣ 150 grams of rigatoni pasta

♣ 2 eggs

♣ 125 grams of mozzarella

♣ 250 grams of bechamel

♣ 1 hectogram of cooked ham

♣ 50 grams of grated parmesan cheese

Preparation"

Boil the pasta and, when it's "al dente" drain it and put it in a large bowl. Next add the boiled eggs (chopped into small pieces), diced mozzarella, chopped ham, and half of the béchamel and parmesan. Pour everything into a buttered Pyrex pan and make sure the mixture has leveld. Then add remaining béchamel (if your cholesterol allows it) and a few flakes of butter. Cook in the oven at the maximum temperature for 20 minutes and then grill for 5 minutes.

Four cheese penne pasta

Ingredients:

* 30 grams of butter
* 1 hectogram of soft cheese
* 30 grams of Parmesan cheese

Preparation"

Add 30 grams of butter and two tablespoons of cooking cream to a large bowl. Next, add cheeses to your liking, as long as can melt when heated, Be sure to cut the cheese into small pieces so they can melt in a few seconds. Drain the penne and pour it over the cheese. Add plenty of grated parmesan and mix with a wooden spatula while it's warm. I recommend you serve this dish very warm.

Penne with cooked ham

Difficoltà   ✗✗✗✗

Tempo   🕐🕐🕐🕐

Costo   💰💰💰💰

Ingredients:

♣ 2 ounces of pennette pasta

♣ 1 hectogram of cooked ham

♣ 125 grams of cream

♣ 30 grams of butter

Preparation:

Fry the diced ham in butter on low heat. When it starts to change color turn off the burner and add cooked and drained pasta. Next, add cream, stir well, and plate.

Penne with ricotta

Difficoltà ✗✗✗✗

Tempo ◷◷

Costo 💰 💰

Ingredients:

* 30 grams of butter
* 2 ounces of ricotta
* 2 ounces of pasta
* Black pepper

Preparation:

Put 30 grams of butter in a bowl and leave it at room temperature for a while. When its soft add 200 grams of ricotta and mix with a fork well. Then add the cooked pasta with a bit of the pasta water. The pasta water is essential for the success of this dish. Mix well with a wooden spatula, plate, sprinkle with plenty of black pepper.

Penne with saffron

Difficoltà ✗✗✗

Tempo 🕐🕐🕐

Costo 💰💰

Ingredients:

- ♣ 2 ounces of pennette pasta
- ♣ 1 hectogram of ricotta
- ♣ 125 grams of cream
- ♣ 30 grams of butter
- ♣ 30 grams of parmesan cheese
- ♣ salt and pepper

Preparation:

While the pasta is boiling, add a dozen saffron stems to a small glass with four tablespoons of warm water. In a bowl add butter (room termperature), cream and ricotta and mix well with a wooden spoon. Drain the pasta and pour it into the sauce. Add the glass with the water and saffron, stir again, and plate.

Penne with salmon and saffron

Ingredients:

* 1 hectogram of salmon
* 30 grams of butter
* 12 stems of saffron
* 2 tablespoons of cream

Preparation:

Cut 100 grams of smoked salmon into very thin slices and fry in a large pan with 30 grams of butter. While this is cooking add a dozen stems of saffron to a little bit of water. Next, cook and drain the pasta and pour it into the pan. Add the water and saffron mixture and two tablespoons of cooking cream. Mix well over heat with a wooden spoon and serve.

Pennette with vodka

✗✗✗

🕐🕐🕐

💰 💰

Ingredients:

♣ 30 grams of butter

♣ 1 half a glass of vodka

♣ 2 tablespoons of cream

♣ 2 ounces of pennette pasta

Preparation:

Melt two pieces butter in a pan. When the butter begins to brown add a half a glass of vodka and turn up the heat. When it starts to boil, take a large lit wooden toothpick (like those used to make skewers) and add it to the pan. This will develop a big flame due to evaporation alcohol which will last, depending on how much vodka you've added, about half a minute or so. As soon as the flame goes out remove the toothpick and pour the penne al dente and two tablespoons of cream into the pot. Add some pepper and serve warm.

Four cheese pizza

✗✗✗✗

🕐🕐🕐🕐

💰 💰

Ingredients:

♣ 200 grams of flour

♣ 7 grams of brewer's yeast

♣ 100 grams of mozzarella

♣ 100 grams of fontina

♣ 100 grams of gorgonzola

♣ 100 grams of provolone

♣ 2 eggs

♣ oil to taste

Preparation:

Put the flour in a bowl and add the dissolved yeast a drop of water and a pinch of salt. Slowly, add half a glass of water and knead with your hands. Once kneaded, create a ball and put the dough aside. After 2 hours shape the dough into two pizza of the thickness you prefer. Top with chopped cheeses and a tablespoon of oil and bake for 10 minutes.

Pizza with croutons

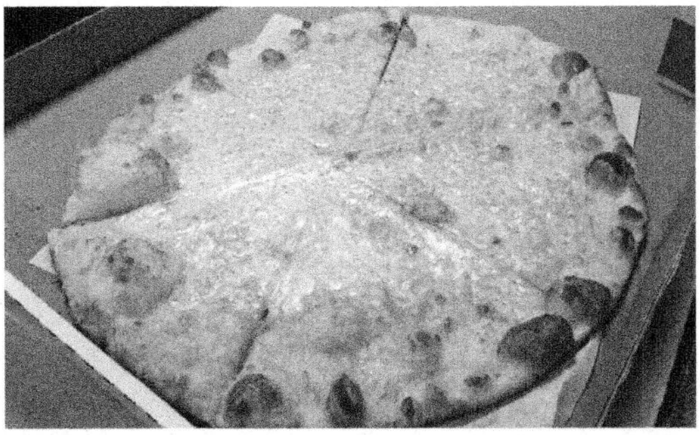

Ingredients:

♣ 200 grams of flour

♣ 7 grams of brewer's yeast

♣ 125 grams of mozzarella

♣ 100 grams of ham

♣ oil to taste

Preparation:

Put the flour in a bowl and add the dissolved yeast a drop of water and a pinch of salt. Slowly, add half a glass of water and knead with your hands. Once kneaded, create a ball and put the dough aside. After 2 hours shape the dough into two pizzas of the thickness you prefer. Top with sliced ham and crumbled mozzarella and cook it in the oven for 10 minutes.

Pizza capricciosa

✗✗✗✗
🕐🕐🕐🕐
💰 💰 💰

Ingredients:

♣ 200 grams of flour

♣ 7 grams of brewer's yeast

♣ 125 grams of mozzarella

♣ 100 grams of ham

♣ 100 grams of salami

♣ 2 eggs

♣ oil to taste

Preparation:

Put the flour in a bowl and add the dissolved yeast a drop of water and a pinch of salt. Slowly, add half a glass of water and knead with your hands. Once kneaded, create a ball and put the dough aside. After 2 hours shape the dough into two pizza of the thickness you prefer. Top with shredded mozzarella, ham, salami, and sliced hard-boiled egg. Drizzle over a heaping tablespoon of oil and put in the oven for 10 minutes.

Pizza alla carbonara

✕✕✕✕
🕐🕐🕐🕐
💰 💰

Ingredients:

- ♣ 200 grams of flour
- ♣ 7 grams of brewer's yeast
- ♣ 125 grams of mozzarella
- ♣ 100 grams of bacon
- ♣ 2 eggs
- ♣ oil to taste

Preparation:

Put the flour in a bowl and add the dissolved yeast a drop of water and a pinch of salt. Slowly, add half a glass of water and knead with your hands. Once kneaded, create a ball and put the dough aside. After 2 hours shape the dough into two pizza of the thickness you prefer. Top with shredded mozzarella, bacon, and an egg in the center. Drizzle with a heaping tablespoon of oil and put in the oven for 10 minutes.

Ravioli with ricotta

⚒⚒⚒⚒

🕐🕐🕐🕐

💰💰💰

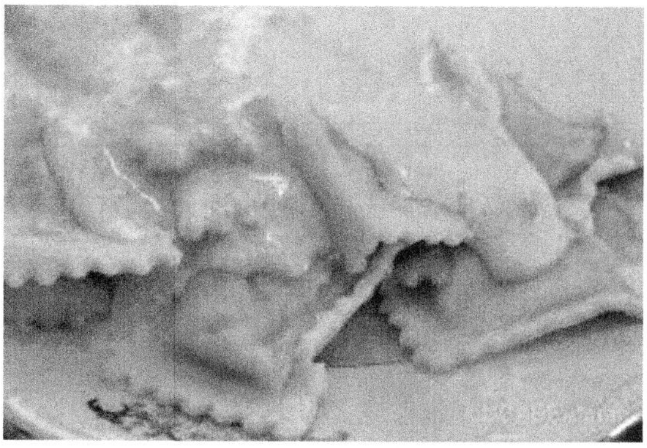

Ingredients:

- ♣ 200 grams of pasta
- ♣ 2 eggs
- ♣ 200 grams of ricotta
- ♣ 100 grams of grated parmesan cheese
- ♣ salt, walnuts

Preparation:

Use a glass to cut circles from the dough and put aside. Next, mix the ricotta with a couple of tablespoons of hot water in a bowl. Slowly incorporate the egg, the Parmesan cheese, a pinch of salt, and a little bit of grated nutmeg. Put a spoonful of the mixture in the center of each disc of dough and close into half-moon shapes. Close the edges well with a fork and boil in water with salt. When they are cooked, drain and season with butter and parmesan.

Rigatoni with lemon

Ingredients:

- ♣ 2 ounces of tagliolini pasta
- ♣ 30 grams of butter
- ♣ 2 lemons

Preparation:

Melt 30 grams of butter and two tablespoons of extra virgin olive oil in a large pan. Grate the peel of two lemons. Turn the burner off and add the lemon peel to the butter and oil. Mix everything with a wooden spoon. Cook and drain (not fully) the tagliolini and pour them into the mixture you prepared. Mix well and serve immediately.

Rigatoni with sausage and cream

Ingredients:

- ♣ 2 minced sausages
- ♣ 200 grams of rigatoni
- ♣ 200 ml of cream
- ♣ 1 half a glass of white wine
- ♣ Black pepper

Preparation:

Cut each of the sausages into small pieces and cook them in the wine. As they cook, they should release fat. At this point, turn the burner to low and continue cooking. Cook and drain the rigatoni (or other pasta of your choice) once it is "al dente". Add it to the pan with sausage and pour and continue cooking for a minute. Then add the cream and stir everything well with a wooden spoon. Top with black pepper and serve.

Rice with milk

⚒⚒⚒

🕐🕐🕐

💰💰

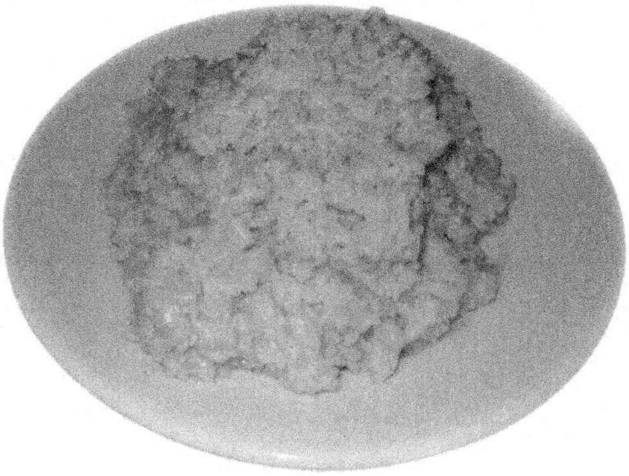

Ingredients:

♣ 160 grams of rice

♣ 1 half a liter of milk

♣ 1 egg

♣ 30 grams of parmesan cheese

Preparation:

Mix half a glass of milk and half a glass of water together and bring to a boil. Add rice and cook, adding the remaining milk gradually. Once the rice is creamy and cooked add the egg yolk, mix well, and add the parmesan. Plate and serve.

Veal risotto

⚒⚒⚒

🕐🕐🕐🕐

💰💰

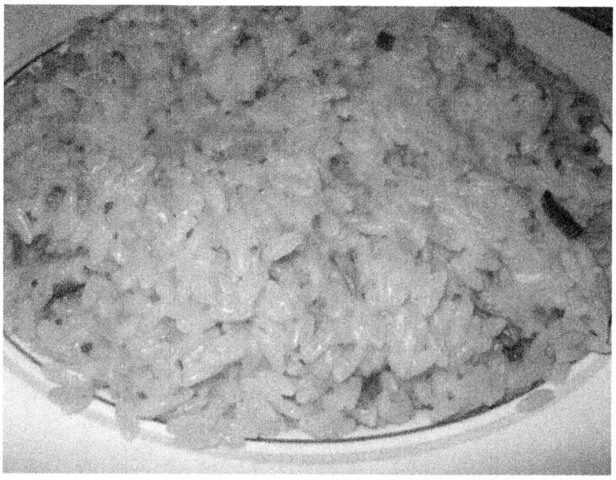

Ingredients:

♣ 3 ounces of lean veal

♣ 160 grams of rice

♣ 1 apple

♣ 1 tablespoon of flour

♣ 2 glasses of broth

♣ 1 half lemon

♣ 50 grams of butter

Preparation:

Cut an apple into thin slices and brown in butter. Cut the veal into small pieces and add to the apples to brown. Slowly add flour to the mixture and cook for an hour and a half. At the end, add the lemon juice. Meanwhile, boil, drain, and rinse the rice and put it in the oven at a high temperature for a few mintues. Take it out of the oven and plate it, making a small crater in the center of the rice. Add the meat and sauce to the middle of the rice and serve.

Smoked risotto

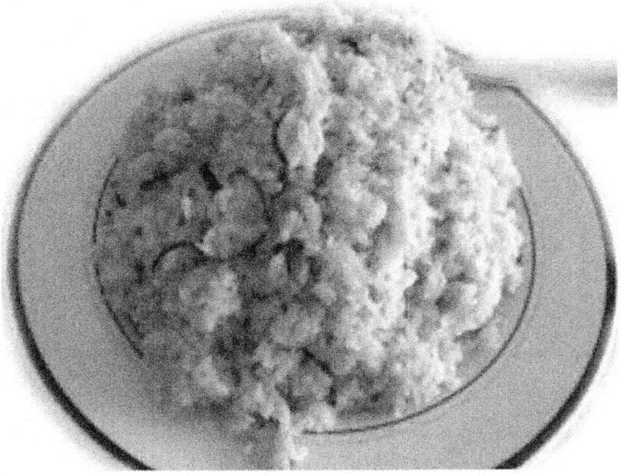

Ingredients:

♣ 160 grams of arborio rice

♣ 50 grams of butter

♣ 125 grams of cream

♣ 1 half nutmeg

♣ 1 hectogram of smoked salmon

♣ 1 hectogram of smoked provola

♣ 1 glass of dry sparkling wine

Preparation:

Warm the butter in a Pyrex dish. Add the rice and fry with chopped salmon. Slowly add the boiling broth and the sparkling wine, stirring constantly. When the risotto is creamy and cooked, turn off the heat and add the smoked provolone in small pieces. Stir until creamy, plate, and serve.

Risotto with castelmagno

✗✗✗✗

🕐🕐🕐🕐

💰💰💰💰

Ingredients:

- ♣ 160 grams of arborio rice
- ♣ 50 grams of butter
- ♣ half nutmeg
- ♣ 1 hectogram of castelmagno
- ♣ 50 grams of grated parmesan cheese

Preparation:

Warm the butter in a Pyrex dish and add the rice to sauté. Slowly add the boiling broth, stirring constantly (do not make the broth too concentrated). When the risotto is cooked it might be a little bland as the castelmagno (full flavor) has not been added. Once it is cooked, turn off the heat and add the chopped castelmagno cheese and the grated parmesan. Mix very well and serve.

Orange risotto

⚒⚒⚒

🕐🕐🕐

💰💰

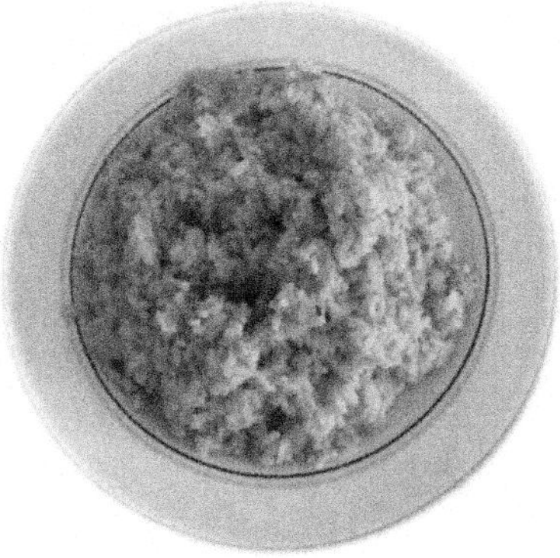

Ingredients:

- ♣ 160 grams of arborio rice
- ♣ 15 grams of orange peel
- ♣ 1 orange juice
- ♣ 1 glass of cognac
- ♣ 1 half nut

Preparation:

Warm the butter in a Pyrex dish and add the rice to sauté in cognac. Slowly add the boiling broth, stirring constantly. When the risotto is cooked and creamy turn off the heat and add the orange zest and orange juice. Take off the burner and mix well. Serve and enjoy.

Rice with beer

✗✗✗✗

🕐🕐🕐🕐

💰💰💰💰

Ingredients:

- ♣ 160 grams of arborio rice
- ♣ 50 grams of butter
- ♣ 125 grams of cream
- ♣ 1 half nutmeg
- ♣ 50 grams of swiss cheese
- ♣ 1 bottle of dark beer

Preparation:

Warm the butter in a Pyrex dish and add the rice to fry. Slowly add the boiling broth and beer, stirring constantly. When the risotto his cooked and creamy, turn off the heat and add the cream and grated swiss cheese. Take off the burner and mix well. Serve and enjoy.

Risotto with Milanese style

🛠🛠🛠🛠

🕐🕐🕐🕐

💰💰

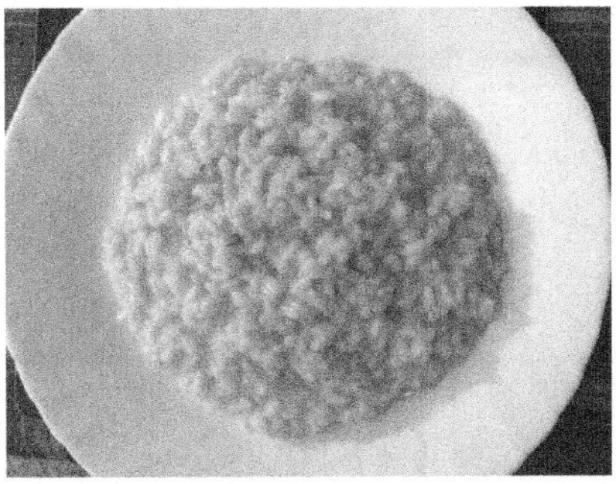

Ingredients:

- ♣ 160 grams of arborio rice
- ♣ 30 grams of butter
- ♣ 1 half a liter of broth
- ♣ 15 stems of saffron or 1 sachet

Preparation:

Brown 30 grams of butter in a Pyrex saucepan. As soon as it's melted add 160 grams of arborio rice, stir with a wooden spoon, making sure that it does not stick to the saucepan. Using a a flame breaker under the dish can help with this. As soon as it starts to become golden, add a few tablespoons of broth. Make sure that it does not boil, burn, or stick to the bottom. Continue to stir it until cooked (about 20 minutes). When cooked add the saffron, a bit of butter, and grated parmesan cheese. Keep on the heat and stir with the wooden spoon for a minute. Serve warm.

Rice with sausage

Ingredients:

- 160 grams of arborio rice
- 1 sausage
- 1 glass of white wine
- Black pepper

Preparation:

Cut the sausage into small pieces and sautee in the wine. As they, cook the fat should melt. Add the rice and cook in the sausage fat at a low temperature, continuously adding water to prevent it from sticking to the sides of the pot. It should be cooked in about 20 minutes. Once cooked, taste and add salt if necessary. Add some black pepper and serve.

Seafood risotto

⚒⚒⚒⚒

🕐🕐🕐🕐🕐

💰💰💰💰

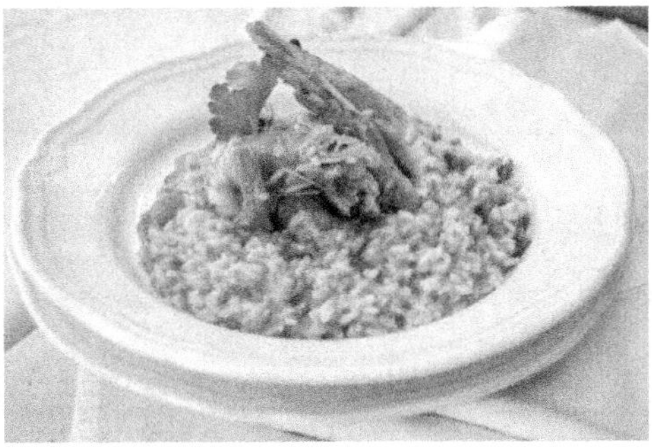

Ingredients:

- ♣ 160 grams of arborio rice
- ♣ 3 ounces of clams
- ♣ 3 ounces of mussels
- ♣ 2 ounces of squid
- ♣ 2 ounces of shrimp
- ♣ ½ fish cube
- ♣ ½ glass of white wine
- ♣ 2 tablespoons of oil
- ♣ 1 clove of garlic

Preparation:

Rinse the clams and mussels well, put in a pot, bring to a boil, and cover. As soon as they open, turn off the heat, and keep covered. Cut the squid into small pieces and fry in a large pot in oil. Once they start to fry, turn the heat down and cover. Cook for ten minutes, adding a little bit of wine if necessary. Next, add the peeled shrimp and continue cooking for another five minutes. Then add the rice and the ½ fish cube and stir with a wooden spoon. When it starts to dry pour in the remaining wine. After cooking for 10 minutes, add the clams and mussels (with the liquid from cooking) to the rice. Continue cooking for another 10 minutes, always adding water when necessary. Serve and enjoy.

Risotto with black sauce

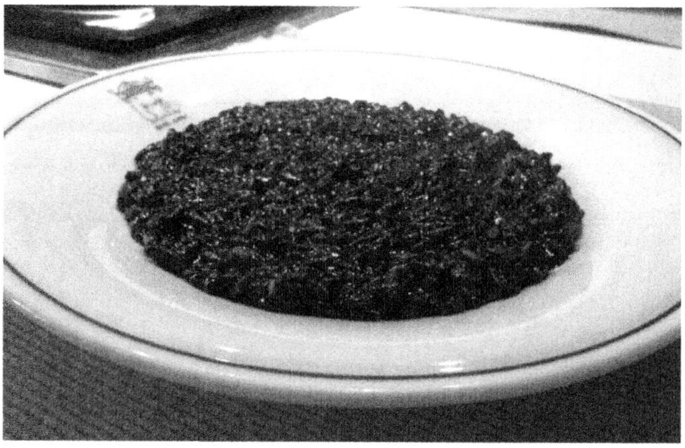

Ingredients:

- ♣ 160 grams of arborio rice
- ♣ 200 grams of cuttlefish
- ♣ 30 grams of butter
- ♣ 2 tablespoons of oil
- ♣ 1 clove of garlic
- ♣ ½ nutmeg
- ♣ ½ glass of white wine

Preparation:

Clean the cuttlefish (setting aside the parts with ink). Cut the cuttlefish into strips and fry in garlic and oil. Add the wine and cook (without a lid). As soon as the wine has evaporated, add a little broth, and put the lid back on to cook for an hour. Once it is cooked, pour the rice and the cuttlefish ink (set aside earlier) into the pot. Add boiling water slowly and cook. When it is cooked add butter and serve.

Spaghetti with garlic, chili pepper and olive oil

✗✗
🕐🕐
💰 💰

Ingredients:

- ♣ 2 ounces of spaghetti
- ♣ 4 tablespoons of oil
- ♣ 4 cloves of garlic
- ♣ 2 tablespoons of breadcrumbs

Preparation:

Pour plenty of extra virgin olive oil into a pan, add four cloves of garlic, and fry on low heat until you see that the garlic starts to turn golden. Cook and drain the spaghetti and add to the pan. Sprinkle in two spoons of breadcrumbs and stir with a wooden ladle. Be sure they do not dry out too much. You can add a few tablespoons of pasta water, if necessary, to thicken. Serve warm and enjoy.

Spaghetti with provolone

Ingredients:

- ♣ 2 ounces of pennette pasta
- ♣ 1 hectogram of provolone
- ♣ 125 grams of cream
- ♣ 30 grams of butter
- ♣ 1 half tablespoon of flour
- ♣ salt and pepper

Preparation:

Melt the butter in a pan on very low heat. Add the flour and cream and mixed. Next, cut provolone cheese into small pieces and add to the pan. Lightly salt and pepper. Cook and drain the penne pasta and pour the sauce over. Sti well and serve hot.

Spaghetti with bottarga

✗✗
🕐🕐
💰💰💰💰

Ingredients:

- ♣ 2 ounces of spaghetti
- ♣ 100 grams of bottarga
- ♣ 2 cloves of garlic
- ♣ 2 tablespoons of extra virgin olive oil

Preparation:

Fry the garlic with oil in a pan on very low heat. Be careful that it does not burn. Cook and drain the pasta when it is al dente. Take the pan off the heat and add the pasta and bottarga. Stir well, adding a few tablespoons of the water from cooking the pasta. Serve and enjoy.

Spaghetti alla carbonara

Difficoltà   ✗ ✗ ✗ ✗

Tempo   🕐🕐🕐

Costo   💰 💰

Ingredients:

- 1 hectogram of bacon
- 1 tablespoon of oil
- ½ glass of white wine
- 2 eggs
- 30 grams of parmesan cheese

Preparation:

Fry one hundred grams of guanciale in a pan on low heat with a tablespoon of olive oil. Add a half glass of dry white wine. The fat of the guanciale should be almost melted on very low heat. While the pasta and bacon cook, separate the egg whites from the yolks. Put the yolks aside and beat the egg whites with a whisk. (Be sure to use a whisk. If you use a fork similar, the egg white will not incorporate enough air which is what makes it soft). Take the pan off the burner and add the pasta. Next, add the yolk, beaten egg white, parmesan, and black pepper. Stir well to mix everything and plate.

Spaghetti with clams

✗✗✗✗
🕐🕐🕐
💰💰💰💰

Ingredients:

- ♣ ½ kilo of clams
- ♣ 3 tablespoons of oil
- ♣ 1 clove of garlic
- ♣ ½ glass of white wine
- ♣ 2 ounces of spaghetti

Preparation:

Carefully wash a half kilo of clams. Put in a strainer to drain for an hour and add salt. Add them to large pan with three tablespoons of olive oil, a clove of garlic, and half a glass of dry white wine. Turn up the heat and cover with a lid. After a few minutes they should open. Now, lower the heat and cook for 4 minutes. Now add spaghetti (al dente) into the pan and stir with a wooden ladle. The spaghetti should finish cooking in the pan. To do this you can add a spoonful of pasta water until the sauce is creamy. Sprinkle with chopped parsley, remove the garlic, and serve.

Tagliolini with sea bass

⚒⚒⚒⚒

🕐🕐🕐🕐

💰💰💰💰

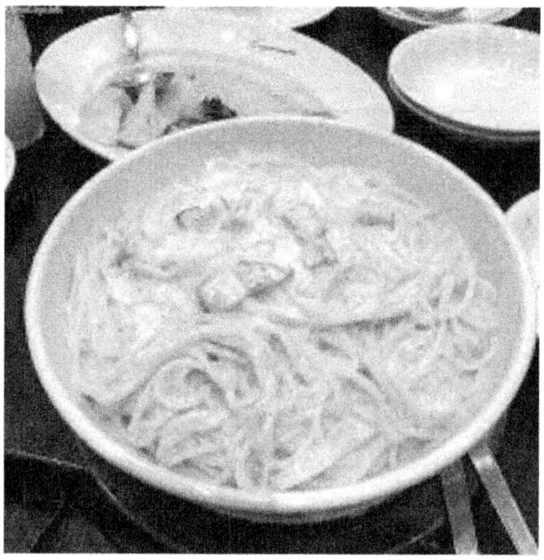

Ingredients:

- ♣ 1 nice sea bass
- ♣ 30 grams of butter
- ♣ 1 cloves of garlic
- ♣ 2 ounces of pasta

Preparation:

Remove any thorns or bones from the fillet of sea bass with fork and sharp knife. Chop it into small pieces. Melt 30 grams of butter in a pan and add a clove of garlic and the chopped sea bass. As soon as the garlic starts to turn golden, remove it. Brown the sea bass and add the cooked and drained pasta al dente. Keep the water from cooking the pasta. Stir for a minute with a wooden spoon, adding a few tablespoons of pasta water, if necessary, to thicken. Sprinkle with parsley and serve.

Tortellini from Bologna

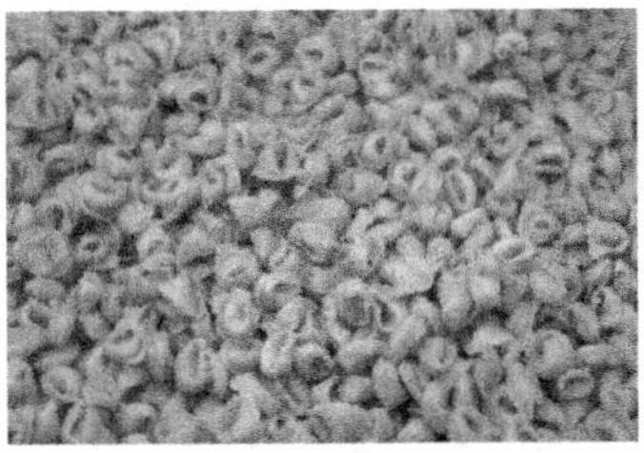

Ingredients:

- ♣ 50 grams of butter
- ♣ 1 pound of lean pork
- ♣ 1 glass of white wine
- ♣ 1 hectogram of mortadella
- ♣ 50 grams of grated parmesan cheese
- ♣ 3 ounces of puffed pastry dough

Preparation:

Melt 50 grams of butter in a pan. When it begins to fry add one hundred grams of chicken breast (cut into pieces) and one hundred grams of lean pork. Gradually add white wine. Make sure it does not burn. Put the cooked meat, a pound of mortadella (cut into pieces), and 50 grams of grated parmesan cheese into a blender and blend well. At this point we need the sheet of puffed pasta. It is easiest to use the premade type from the grocery store. Roll out the puffed pastry on a floured board and use a glass take a glass to make circles from the dough. Add a spoon of the meat mixture to the center of each piece of puffed pastry. At this point we must close the cappelletti. First, we lightly grease the outside rim of the circles with the beaten egg using your finger. This will help to make the dough adhesive. Now fold the circle in half and, with the help of a fork, pinch the edges together. While you are folding the circle keep a finger in the center to obtain the characteristic shape of the tortellino. Boil the tortellini in plenty of water and season to your liking with butter and cream or meat sauce. You can also cook the tortellini directly in meat broth.

Potato soup

X X X X

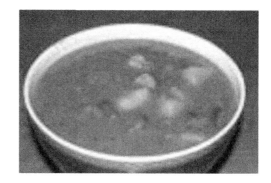

Ingredients:

* ♣ 1 liter of broth
* ♣ 4 potatoes
* ♣ 1 hectogram of cream
* ♣ 15 grams of butter
* ♣ nutmeg

Preparation:

Cut the potatoes into pieces and boil them in the broth. When cooked, mash the pototoes and put back on low heat. Add the butter, cream, and parmesan cheese. Mix with a wooden spoon, plate, and sprinkle with nutmeg.

main dishes

Fried lamb

✗✗✗

◷◷◷

💰 💰 💰 💰

Ingredients:

* 8 lamb cutlets
* 1 hectogram of breadcrumbs
* 1 egg
* oil, salt and pepper

Preparation:

Beat the egg in a bowl and add pinch of salt. Dip the cutlets inside, covering each in egg and cover in breadcrumbs. If the breadcrumbs are not sticking well, use your hands to press them into the cutlets. Heat oil in a large pan and, once hot, add the cutlets. Once they start to turn golden, flip them. Once cooked, lower the heat and continue cooking for several minutes to make sure the inside is cooked. Plate and enjoy.

Lamb chops

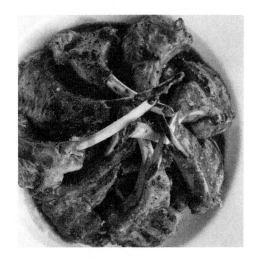

Ingredients:

- ♣ 8 lamb cutlets
- ♣ oil, salt and pepper

Preparation:

Heat oil in a pan and once it is hot, add the cutlets. Once they start to change color, fip and cook the other side. Once both sides are browned, lower the heat and continue cooking for several minutes to make sure the inside is cooked.

Baked lamb

⚒⚒⚒⚒

🕐🕐🕐🕐

💰💰💰💰

Ingredients:

- ♣ 1 leg of lamb (about 1 kg)
- ♣ 3 cloves of garlic
- ♣ 2-3 grams of thyme
- ♣ olive oil
- ♣ ½ kilo of potatoes
- ♣ salt and pepper

Preparation:

Take the lamb out of the the refrigerator 1 hour before you want to start cooking. Preheat the oven to 240 °C. In a bowl, mix the olive oil, thyme and crushed garlic. Coat the lamb generously with this mixture, rubbing the meat with your fingers to make sure the breading herbs stick. Bake the lamb in the oven for 15 minutes on high heat. Then lower the oven temperature to 200 °C. Drizzle with a bit of olive oil and sprinkle the surface with a pinch of salt as it cooks. Add the washed and cut potatoes around the meat and cook for 25 minutes. Once cooked, remove from the oven and cover with foil for 15 minutes. Cut into slices and serve immediately.

Baked anchovies

Ingredients:

- ♣ 4 ounces of anchovies
- ♣ 10 grams of breadcrumbs
- ♣ 1 lemon
- ♣ oil and salt

Preparation:

Cut open the anchovies and remove the head and bones. Greasen a pan, add the cleaned anchovies, and sprinkle with breadcrumbs, oil and salt. Next, make a second layer of anchioves and sprinkle lemon juice over. Then cook in the oven (medium temperature) for fifteen minutes. Once cooked, grill on the stove to brown the outside.

Orange duck in the microwave

Ingredients:

* 250 grams of duck breast
* 1 orange
* 2 tablespoons of oil
* 1 hectogram of flour
* salt and pepper

Preparation:

This is a very simplified version of classic orange duck. It only takes a few minutes, but the result is wonderful. Marinate the sliced meat with oil, orange, salt, and black pepper for two hours. Then, without draining it too much, put the meat on a microwave-safe plate and cook in the microwave for three minutes. Let it cool a little and coat with flour. Put the slices of meat back into the microwave on medium power and cook for 5 to 6 minutes. Plate and glaze with the sauce from cooking.

Pork loin with milk

✗✗✗

🕐🕐🕐🕐

💰💰

Ingredients:

- ♣ ½ kilo pork loin
- ♣ ½ liter of milk
- ♣ 20 grams of butter
- ♣ salt and pepper

Preparation:

Add the meat to a baking dish and brown with butter and pinch of salt and pepper. Turn it often and, when it is well browned on both sides, pour over the milk covering the meat. Cover and cook for about two hours. The milk will make a cream. Cut the pork loin into slices, plate, and top with the milk cream.

Braciato

Difficoltà	✗✗✗✗
Tempo	🕐🕐🕐
Costo	💰 💰 💰

Ingredients:

- ♣ ½ kilo of beef rib
- ♣ 1 hectogram of bacon
- ♣ 1 liter of red wine
- ♣ 4 cloves of garlic

Preparation:

Cut deep incisions in the meat with a sharp knife and stuff with pieces of bacon. Put the meat and garlic in a Pyrex dish and cover with wine. Set aside and let it marinate overnight. The next day, add butter and oil to another pan and heat. Drain and dry the meat with a paper towel and add to the pan. Brown the meat on both sides and add the wine. Cover and cook on low heat for 2 and a half hours.

Bourguignonne meat

✗ ✗ ✗ ✗

🕐 🕐 🕐 🕐

💰 💰 💰 💰

Ingredients:

♣ 1 hectogram of bacon

♣ 2 carrots

♣ 1 tablespoon of oil

♣ 400 grams of beef

♣ 1 bottle of red wine

Preparation:

Cut 100 grams of bacon into cubes. Put the cubes in large pan and add half a glass of water. Partially cover with a lid and cook on very low heat to melt the fat and allow the bacon to brown well. Remove the bacon, drain it, and set it aside. Cut two carrots into cubes and put them in the pan to brown in the bacon fat. If necessary, add a tablespoon of oil. When they are browned, drain, and add to the bacon. Next, take 400 grams of beef. Ideally, it is best to use beef cheek, but it is not always easy to find. Instead, you can use rose of beef, cut it into medium-size cubes. Dry the meat well with a paper towel and flour it with your hands. Slowly, little by little, add the meat to a pan. When the meat is browned, add the carrots and bacon that you have set aside. Raise the heat a bit and then pour a bottle of strong red wine. Turn the burner down and cover well. Cook for three hours on low heat. At this time, the meat should be immersed in an exquisite cream created from the fat of the bacon, the flour, and the evaporated wine. In the original recipe, from France, this dish is accompanied with boiled potatoes or homemade fettuccine with cream as side dishes.

Beef carpaccio

🛠🛠

🕐🕐

💰💰💰💰

Ingredients:

♣ 2 ounces of beef fillet

♣ 1 tablespoon of green pepper

♣ 1 handful of black pepper

♣ 4 tablespoons of oil

♣ 1 hectogram of Parmesan cheese

♣ 1 lemon

Preparation:

Cut the fillet into fine slices and lay out on a dish. In a bowl, add the juice of one lemon, four tablespoons of extra virgin olive oil, coarsely ground black pepper, green peppercorns, parmesan flakes and a pinch of salt. Mix well and pour over the meat. Cover with baking paper and refrigerate for an hour before serving.

Salmon carpaccio

Ingredients:

* 150 grams of smoked salmon
* 1 piece of butter
* 1 lemon
* a bit of pink pepper

Preparation:

Take 150 grams of smoked salmon and put on a plate greased with butter.
Pour over the juice from one lemon and sprinkle with some pink pepper and
some butter curls. Refrigerate for half an hour and serve.

Baked lamb roast leg

✖✖✖✖
🕐🕐🕐🕐
💰💰💰💰

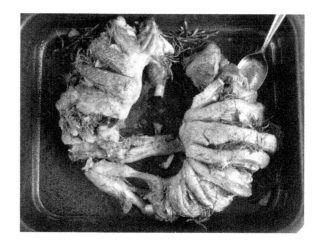

Ingredients:

* 1 leg of lamb
* 2 cloves of garlic
* 1 hectogram of bacon
* 1 liter of red wine
* 1 kilo of potatoes

Preparation:

Make incisions with a sharp knife in the leg of lamb and stuff with pieces of garlic and bacon. Put in a bowl and cover with the wine. Leave it marinating for a few hours together. Meanwhile, cut the potatoes into thick slices. Remove the meat from the wine, dry it and grease it with butter and oil. Do the same thing with the potatoes and then put everything in the oven. Cook slowly, adding the liquid from the marinade to keep the roast from drying out. When cooked, it should be very tender. Serve and enjoy.

Mussels with marinara

✕✕✕✕

🕐🕐🕐

💰 💰

Ingredients:

- ♣ 4 tablespoons of olive oil
- ♣ 1 chili pepper
- ♣ 4 cloves of garlic
- ♣ 1 1/2 kilo of mussels
- ♣ 1 glass of white wine
- ♣ 1 sprig of parsley

Preparation:

In a fairly large pot, add four tablespoons of olive oil, a piece of chilli pepper, and four cloves of garlic. Put on low heat and, after a few minutes, add a kilo and a half of well-cleaned mussels. Cover with a lid to cook. After a few minutes you will see that the mussels will have opened. At this point, add half a glass of white wine and cook for a few more minutes with the lid half open. Once cooked sprinkle with parsley and serve.

Marsala slices

⚒⚒⚒

🕐🕐🕐

💰💰💰

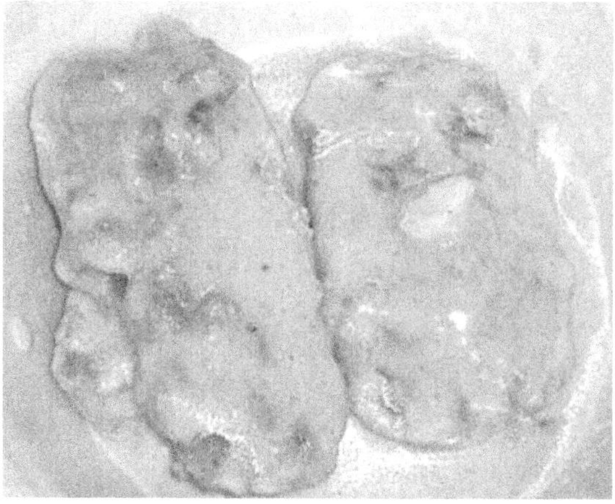

Ingredients:

- ♣ 4 ounces of sliced veal
- ♣ 1 hectogram of flour
- ♣ 1 glass of Marsala wine
- ♣ 50 grams of butter

Preparation:

Dry the slices of meat well and coat them in flour. Melt the butter in a pan and, when it starts to fry, gently add the floured slices of veal. Cook on high heat and, as soon as the meat starts to brown, flip so the other side can cook. When both sides are browned add the marsala wine, lower the heat, and cook for five minutes on each side without a lid.

Cod fillets

🛠🛠🛠🛠

🕐🕐

💰💰

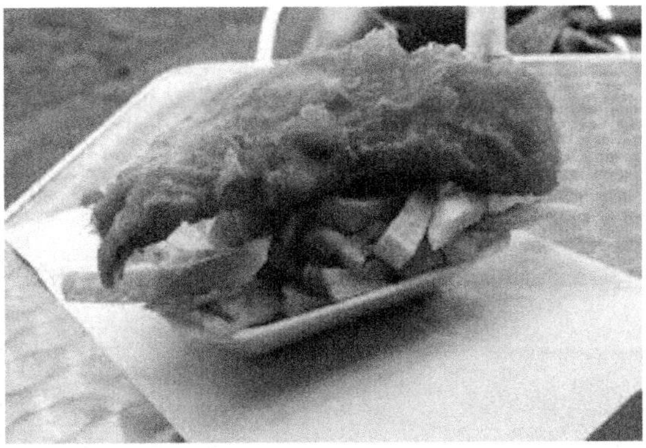

Ingredients:

♣ 1 fillet of cod fish

♣ 2 ounces of flour

♣ a pinch of yeast

♣ lots of oil

Preparation:

Start with a nice fillet weighing about 400 grams. Cut it into four pieces. To make a batter, mix 200 grams of flour, a couple of grams of yeast and enough water to obtain the right consistency. For frying, it would be ideal to have two pots, the first with oil at a high temperature oil and the second, also with oil, but at a lower temperature oil. Dip the pieces of cod in the batter, making sure each is covered. Put each in the warmer (first) pot for a few minutes to allow a thick crust to form. Next, move them to the second pan (lower temperature). This will allow the fish to cook all the way through. Serve warm.

Beef fillet in butter

✗✗✗✗

🕐🕐

💰💰💰💰

Ingredients:

♣ 4 ounces of beef fillet

♣ 40 grams of butter

Preparation:

Soften a piece of butter with your hands and carefully coat two beef fillets weighing 200 grams each. Heat a grill pan on the stove. When it is hot, add the fillets. A "crust" should form, preventing the blood from leaving. Cook on high heat, adding a few flakes of butter every now and then. When you see that the meat comes off from the grill alone, remove it with a spatula and place it on a plate. Wait for the pan heat again on the stove and repeat with the uncooked side of beef. It is important not to touch the meat while it's cooking to avoid liquid leakage. This can make the meat harder and less flavorful. Take the fillets off the stove and while they are still hot, add a few pieces of butter. Sprinkle the fillets with pepper and salt and serve hot.

Beef fillet in salt

✗✗

🕐🕐🕐

💰💰💰💰

Ingredients:

- ♣ 1 ½ kilo fillet of beef
- ♣ 1 kilo of coarse salt
- ♣ half a lemon
- ♣ black pepper
- ♣ 2 tablespoons of oil

Preparation:

Start with the fillet of beef and, with a sharp knife, clean away any fat. Put a sheet of parchment paper on a baking sheet and sprinkle with half of the salt required for this recipe. Place the fillet on top and cover with the remaining salt. Close the paper forming a bag and place in the oven at the maximum temperature for 40 minutes. When it's cooked, break up any pieces of salt, put the fillet on a cutting board and slice it into thick slices. Season with salt, oil and pepper and serve hot.

Valdostana fondue

⚒⚒⚒⚒
🕐🕐🕐🕐
💰💰💰💰

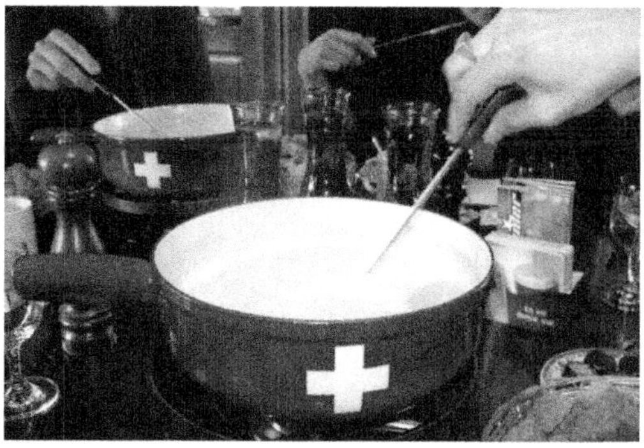

Ingredients:

♣ 2 ounces of fontina cheese

♣ ½ glass of milk ♣ 1 egg

Preparation:

Cut 200 grams of fontina cheese into small pieces and put them in a saucepan with half a glass of milk to soak for at least 2 hours. After 2 hours, put the saucepan on the stove on very low heat and stir continuously with a wooden ladle until the cheese is completely melted. Now, add an egg yolk and continue cooking. Be sure to stir for at least another 30 minutes until the mixture is homogeneous and thick enough. Pour the fondue into small earthenware bowls so that it stays hot. Serve with bread or small croutons for dipping.

Breaded cheese

Ingredients:

- ♣ 2 ounces of soft cheese
- ♣ 1 egg
- ♣ breadcrumbs
- ♣ parmesan
- ♣ oil for frying

Preparation:

Cut the cheese into two centimeters slices and set aside. Beat the egg white in a bowl until stiff. Next, add the yolk and parmesan cheese and beat again. Dip the slices of cheese in the batter and coat with breadcrumbs. Fry in boiling oil and serve hot.

Ham frittata

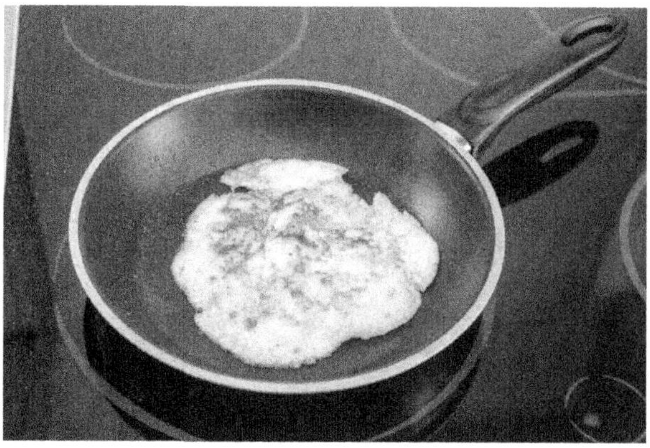

Ingredients:

- ♣ 3 eggs
- ♣ 1 piece mozzarella (125 grams)
- ♣ 60 grams of cooked ham
- ♣ 30 grams of butter

Preparation:

Separate the egg whites and yolks and set the yolks aside. Beat the egg whites until stiff in a bowl with a pinch of salt. Next add the egg yolks, chopped mozzarella, and chopped ham. Melt the butter in a pan and add the egg, cheese, and ham mixture. The mixture should cook for a couple of minutes. Then turn the omelette over and cook on the other side.

Mixed fried fish

✕✕✕✕
🕐🕐🕐
💰💰💰💰

Ingredients:

- ♣ 2 ounces of squid
- ♣ 2 ounces of shrimp
- ♣ 2 ounces of small mullet
- ♣ 2 ounces of small blue fish
- ♣ flour, oil, and lemon

Preparation:

Cut the squid into rings and coat with flour. Repeat with the other seafood. Add enough oil for frying to a deep pan. Turn the burner on high and, when you see that the oil is boiling, add the seafood. After one minute, lower the heat. This will aloow inside of the fish to cook. Now, drain the fish on paper suitable for absorbing the oil. Add salt lemon slices as garnish and serve.

Fish of the poor

⚒⚒⚒

🕐🕐

💰💰

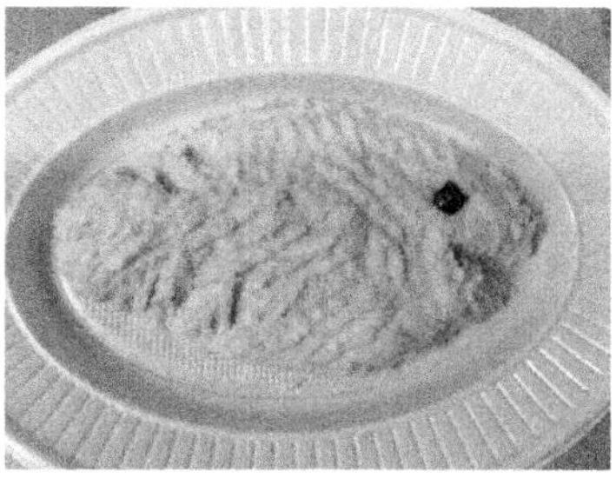

.

Ingredients:

♣ 400 grams of tuna in oil

♣ 200 grams of mayonnaise

♣ 2 capers

Preparation:

Start with 400 grams of excellent quality tuna. In a bowl, pull apart the tuna using a fork and add 200 grams of mayonnaise, a little bit at a time. Mix well and form into the shape of a fish with your hands. You can even use a fork to make fake scales and add the two capers as “eyes”. Put the "fish" in the refrigerator an hour before serving to firm.

Sea Salad

🛠🛠🛠

🕐🕐🕐

💰💰💰

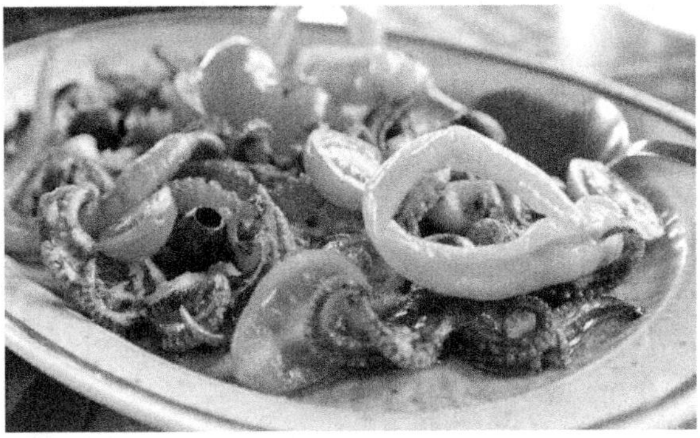

Ingredients:

- ♣ 160 grams of arborio rice
- ♣ 500 grams of mussels
- ♣ 20 grams of prawn tails
- ♣ 300 grams of clams
- ♣ 2 tablespoons of oil
- ♣ 1 clove of garlic
- ♣ 1 lemon
- ♣ ½ glass of white wine

Preparation:

Boil the mussels and clams in a covered pot. As soon as they are all open, drain, and set aside. Be sure to keep the liquid they have produced. Deshell the shellfish and put them in a bowl. Add juice from one lemon and two tablespoons of olive oil. Boil the rice, drain it (al dente), and set it aside to cool. When it is cold, place it in the bowl with the shellfish. Add the liquid from cooking the mussels and clams. Stir well and refrigerate half an hour before serving.

Octopus salad

🛠🛠🛠

🕐🕐🕐

💰💰💰

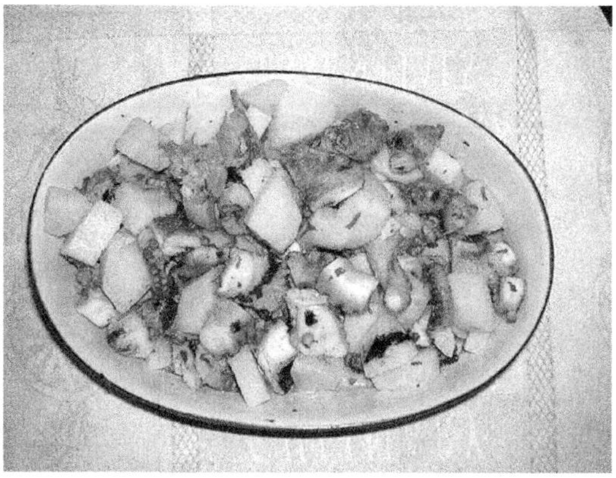

Ingredients:

- ♣ 1 octopus
- ♣ 1 piece of fennel
- ♣ 1 orange
- ♣ salt and pepper

Preparation:

Boil the octopus in water with salt for about forty minutes. Let it cool, clean it well, dry it, and cut it into small pieces. In the meantime, cut the piece of fennel into slices and add it to the octopus. Peel an orange and separate it into wedges. Add this to the rest of the seasoning, oil, salt, and black pepper, and the juice of another orange. Serve. If you'd like you can add boiled potatoes.

Tuna rice salad

Ingredients:

* 160 grams of rice
* 250 grams of canned tuna
* 2 anchovies
* 200 grams of mayonnaise

Preparation:

Boil and drain the rice. Rinse with cold water to remove the starch and add the well-drained and crumbled tuna. Add the mayonnaise and mix well. Garnish with hardboiled eggs and serve cold.

Rolls

❌❌❌
🕐🕐🕐
💰 💰 💰

Ingredients:

- ♣ 4 ounces of veal slices
- ♣ 1 hectogram of mortadella
- ♣ 2 eggs
- ♣ 20 grams of butter
- ♣ 4 tablespoons of oil
- ♣ ½ glass of dry white wine

Preparation:

Beat the eggs (as if you are making an omelette). Add them to a pan with the butter and make very thin omelettes. On top, add a slice of mortadella and layer another omelette on top. Repeat this and roll each and close with a toothpick. Cook in a pan with a piece of butter and 4 tablespoons of oil. Add a drop of wine every now and then.

American rolls

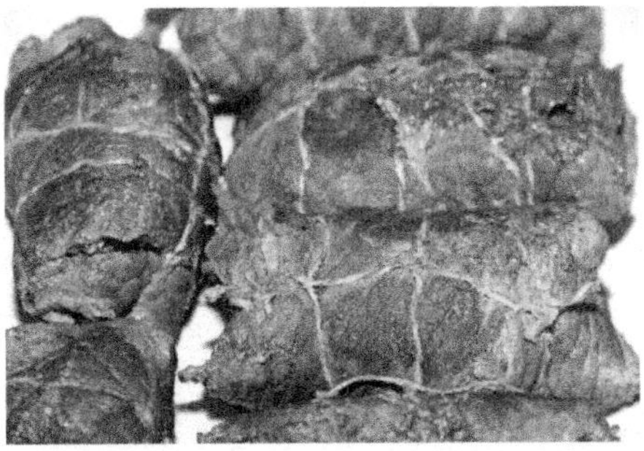

Ingredients:

♣ 6 slices of veal

♣ ½ pineapple

♣ 30 grams of butter

♣ ½ glass of white wine

♣ 2 tablespoons of flour

Preparation:

It is an undisputed back that America is a great technological power. What you might not have known is that US traditions are also important in the kitchen. This is a typical American dish that may be a bit different from what our Italian palates are used to.

Beat the slices of veal with a wooden hammer. Cut the pineapple into six slices and wrap each slice around a piece of meat. Tie the individual rolls with a cooking string, coat them lightly in the flour, and cook them in the butter, slowly adding wine.

Beef boiled meat

✗✗✗

🕐🕐🕐🕐

💰 💰 💰

Ingredients:

♣ ½ kilo of beef

♣ 4 potatoes

♣ salt to your liking

Preparation:

Ask the butcher for a piece of lean beef (suitable for boiled meat) and a nice bone with nerves. Fill a large pot with two liters of water, add a pinch of salt, and the bone and bring to a boil. When the water is at a rolling boil, add the beef. It is important that the water is boiling to maintain the flavor of the meat. In fact, the contact of the meat with the high temperature water transforms the proteins which prevents liquids from leaving the meat. Boil for an hour and a half. Then add four peeled potatoes (not too large) and continue cooking for another half hour. The meat and potatoes can be served either hot or cold. This dish can be seasoned with simple oil, salt and pepper or with various sauces or toppings, such as truffles or mayonnaise.

Pork loin in the microwave

✗✗

🕐🕐

💰 💰 💰

Ingredients:

* 400 grams of pork loin
* 6 slices of lard
* 100 ml of milk
* 100 ml of white wine
* 1 shot of sherry
* 3 tablespoons of oil
* 1 tablespoon of flour
* salt and pepper to taste

Preparation:

Wrap each piece of meat in a slice of lard. Grease with oil and put it in a Pyrex dish. Pour over wine and sherry and cook for ten minutes at maximum heat in the oven. Take it out of the oven and put on a serving plate. Slowly add flour to the cooking juices and mix well with a whisk. Cut the meat into slices, pour the sauce over, serve hot.

Baked pork with apples

⚒⚒

🕐🕐🕐

💰💰💰

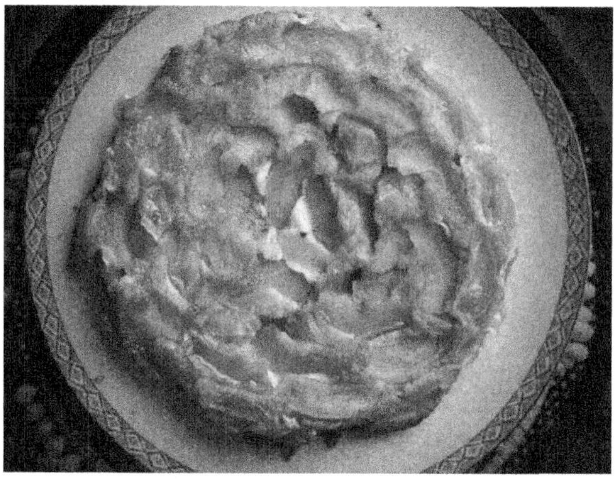

Ingredients:

♣ 400 grams of pork loin

♣ 20 grams of butter

♣ ½ glass of white wine

♣ 2 apples

♣ salt and pepper to taste

Preparation:

Cut the pork loin into fairly thick slices and place them in Pyrex dish greased with butter. Add the wine, cover, and cook in the microwave for 15 minutes at maximum power. Be sure that the meat has cooked and set it aside. Now, cut the apples into thin slices, place them on a microwave-safe dish, cover them with plastic wrap, and cook for 7 to 8 minutes on medium power. Arrange the slices of meat on a serving dish, cover with apple slices, sprinkle with the cooking liquid. Cook in the oven for a minute before serving.

Baked meat

✗✗✗✗
🕐🕐🕐🕐
💰💰💰💰

Ingredients:

* ½ full chicken
* 2 sausages
* 3 ounces of lean veal
* ½ kilo of potatoes
* oil and salt

Preparation:

Grease a Pyrex dish with a bit of oil. Cut the chicken, sausage, and veal into small pieces. Add the the chicken, sausage, and veal to the dish and pour over two tablespoons of oil. Add salt and pepper and put in the oven for half an hour. Then, add two potatoes cut into wedges and cook in the oven for another half hour. Serve and enjoy.

Omelette stuffed

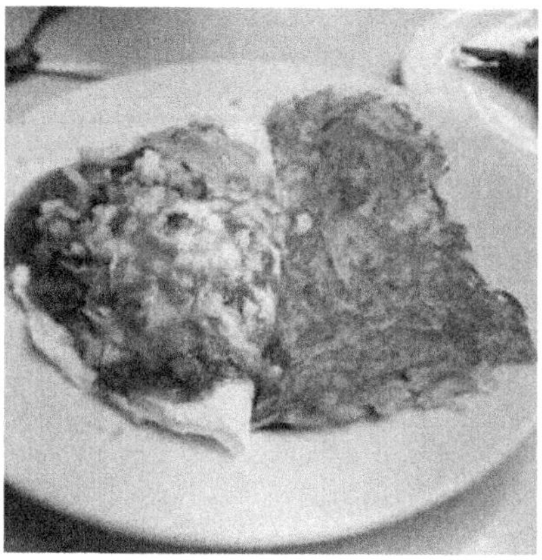

Ingredients:

- 4 eggs
- 1 hectogram of mozzarella
- 1 hectogram of cooked ham
- 20 grams of parmesan cheese
- 30 grams of butter

Preparation:

Cut the mozzarella and ham into small pieces and put aside. Separate the whites from the yolks of four eggs. In a bowl, beat the egg white with a whisk until stiff. Next, add the four yolks and continue to beat until mixed. Melt the butter in a pan, pour in half of the beaten egg mixture and cook for a couple of minutes. At this point put half of the ham and cheese that you have set aside into the center of the omelette. Gently flip over half of the omelette with a spatula to create a bundle with the meat and cheese inside. Cook for three minutes on low heat so that the mozzarella melts and warms. Repeat to create a second omelette.

Ossobuchi alla milanese

✕✕✕
🕐🕐🕐
💰💰💰💰

Ingredients:

♣ 4 veal ossobuchi

♣ 50 grams of butter

♣ 1 hectogram of flour

♣ 1 glass of white wine

Preparation:

Dry the ossobuchi well and coat in flour. Melt butter in a pan and gently put the floured ossobuchi in the pan. Cook on high heat and, as soon as the meat starts to bown, turn it over. When both sides are cooked, add the wine, and lower the heat. Cover with a lid and cook for two hours.

Grilled swordfish

✗✗
🕐🕐
💰💰💰💰

Ingredients:

* 400 grams of swordfish
* 30 grams of butter
* 1 tablespoon of anchovy paste
* salt and pepper

Preparation:

Soften the butter so that it's at room temperature. Put the butter in a bowl and add a spoonful of anchovy paste. Mix well. Coat the two slices of swordfish with the butter mixture. Grill for two minutes on each side. Be sure not to cook longer. Garnish with lemon slices.

Chicken breast with lemon

Ingredients:

* ♣ 2 chicken breasts
* ♣ 1 hectogram of flour
* ♣ 2 lemons
* ♣ 50 grams of butter
* ♣ salt and pepper

Preparation:

Cut the chicken breast into thin slices, dry them with a paper towel. and coat it in flower. Pan fry in butter, gradually adding the lemon juice. Be sure to flip the chicken breasts several times until they are browned. Serve with a few slices of lemon for garnish.

Chicken breast with wine

✗✗✗

🕐🕐🕐

💰 💰

Ingredients:

- ♣ 2 chicken breasts
- ♣ 1 hectogram of flour
- ♣ 1 glass of white wine
- ♣ 50 grams of butter
- ♣ 1 lemon
- ♣ salt and pepper

Preparation:

Cut the chicken breast into thin slices, dry them with a paper towel. and coat it in flower. Pan fry in butter, gradually adding the white wine. Be sure to flip the chicken breasts several times until they are browned. Serve with a few slices of lemon for garnish.

Chicken cacciatore

✗✗✗
🕐🕐🕐
💰💰

Ingredients:

- ½ full chicken
- 2 cloves of garlic
- ½ glass of white wine
- oil, salt and pepper

Preparation:

Cut the chicken into pieces. Add two tablespoons of oil and two cloves of garlic in a pan to fry. Add the chicken and brown well on high heat. When the chicken is browned, add the wine, reduce the heat, and cover with a lid. Continue cooking on medium heat for an hour.

Chicken Marengo

🛠🛠🛠🛠

🕐🕐🕐🕐

💰💰

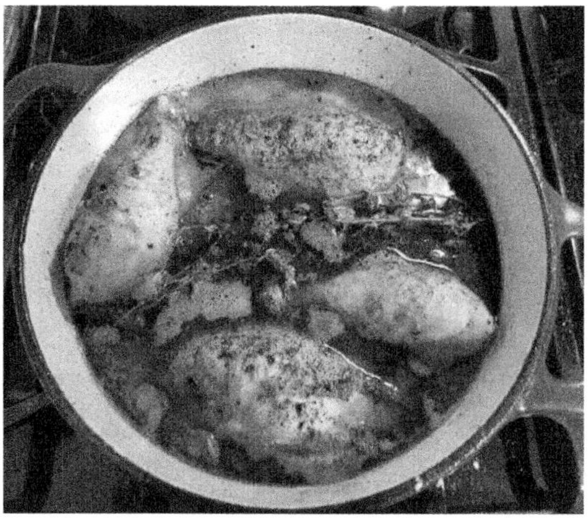

Ingredients:

- ½ full chicken
- 30 grams of butter
- 1 tablespoon of flour
- ½ glass of white wine
- ½ liter of meat broth

Preparation:

Cut the chicken into pieces and brown it in a saucepan with the butter. When browned, gradually add the wine and flour. Once it has congealed, add the broth, put the lid on, and cook for an hour before serving. Plate the chicken, pour over the gravy, and add a squeezed lemon.

Boneless chicken

⚒⚒⚒⚒

🕐🕐🕐🕐

💰💰💰💰

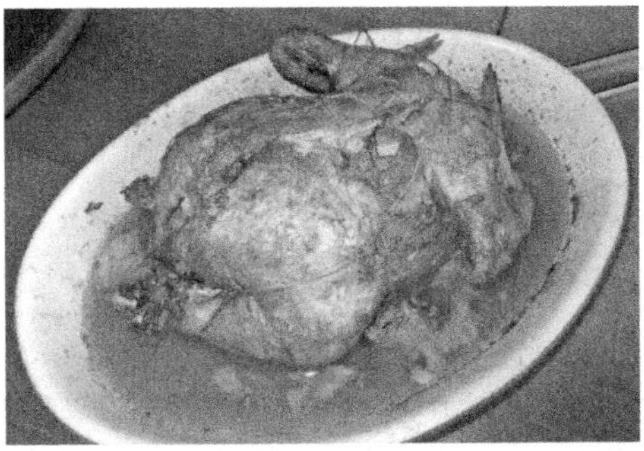

Ingredients:

- ♣ 1 full chicken
- ♣ 50 grams of parmesan cheese
- ♣ 3 hard-boiled eggs
- ♣ 1 hectogram of fontina cheese
- ♣ 1 hectogram of cooked ham
- ♣ 1 handful of breadcrumbs

Preparation:

Ask the butcher to debone a chicken. In a bowl, add the grated Parmesan cheese, the fontina cheese (cut into cubes), two hard-boiled eggs (cut into slices), and the diced cooked ham. Next add the breadcrumbs and a whole raw egg and stir the mixture well. Next, fill the chicken with the mixture and sew it closed chicken needle and thread. Boil it in water with salt for two hours. Once cooked, the chicken must be cooled, preferably in the fridge, and cut into slices.

Fried chicken

✖✖✖✖

🕐🕐🕐🕐

💰💰💰💰

Ingredients:
- ♣ ½ full chicken
- ♣ 2 cloves of garlic
- ♣ 3 hard-boiled eggs
- ♣ 1 hectogram of breadcrumbs
- ♣ 1 egg
- ♣ oil, salt, and pepper

Preparation:

Cut the chicken into pieces. Put the pieces in a bowl and with oil, salt, pepper, and the juice of one lemon. Set aside and let it rest for an hour. Beat an egg in a dish. Dip each piece of chicken in the beaten egg and then coat with breadcrumbs. Pan fry on high heat, turning with a wooden spoon until they are well browned on both sides. Turn down the heat and continue cooking until the chicken is fully cooked.

Meatballs in the pan

⚒⚒⚒

🕐🕐🕐🕐

💰💰💰

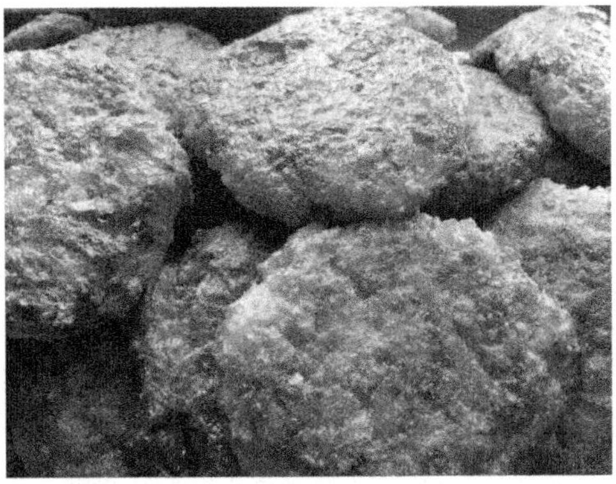

Ingredients:

- ♣ 3 ounces of minced lean veal
- ♣ 1 hectogram of cooked or raw ham
- ♣ 1 egg
- ♣ 30 grams of parmesan cheese
- ♣ 2 tablespoons of oil
- ♣ 30 grams of butter

Preparation:

Mix minced meat and minced ham (cooked or raw to your liking). Next, add a whole raw egg and Parmesan cheese and mix well. Use the mixture to make small meatballs. Cook in a pan oil and butter.

Meatballs impanate

✗✗✗✗

🕐🕐🕐🕐

💰💰💰💰

Ingredients:

- ♣ 3 ounces of minced lean veal
- ♣ 1 hectogram of cooked or raw ham
- ♣ 2 eggs
- ♣ 30 grams of Parmesan cheese
- ♣ 2 tablespoons of oil
- ♣ 30 grams of butter
- ♣ 1 hectogram of breadcrumbs

Preparation:

Mix minced meat and minced ham (cooked or raw to your liking). Next, add a whole raw egg and Parmesan cheese and mix well. Use the mixture to make small meatballs. Dip each meatball in egg and then coat in breadcrumbs. Cook in a pan oil and butter.

Veal roulade

✗✗✗✗
🕐🕐🕐🕐
💰💰💰💰

Ingredients:

- ♣ ½ kilo of veal rump
- ♣ 2 eggs
- ♣ 1 hectogram of cooked ham
- ♣ ½ glass of wine
- ♣ 30 grams of grated parmesan cheese

Preparation:

Start by making a simple omelette with the two eggs. Then spread the veal rump on a baking sheet and place the omelette on top. Next, add the cooked ham on top and sprinkle with grated parmesan cheese. Now wrap the rump into a roll making sure it does not loose any filling. Use a cooking string to tie the roll closed for cooking. To cook start my browing a clove of garlic in a pan with two tablespoons of olive oil and a piece of butter. As soon as the garlic is golden, add the roll to brown. Once it has a nice color add the wine, cover, and cook for an hour and a half.

Sausages with roast potatoes

🛠🛠🛠

🕐🕐🕐

💰💰

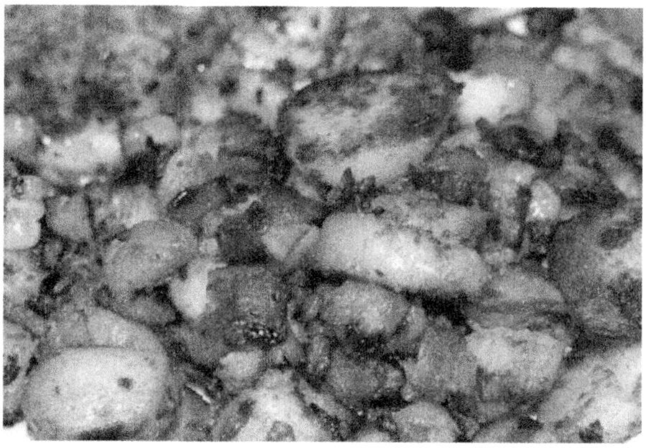

Ingredients:

♣ 4 sausages

♣ 4 potatoes

♣ 1 clove of garlic

♣ 2 tablespoons of oil

♣ 1 sprig of rosemary

Preparation:

Lightly grease a Pyrex container and add four sausages (cut into pieces), four nice potatoes (cut into pieces- more or less the size of the sausages), a clove of garlic, a sprig of rosemary, two tablespoons of oil, and a small splash of white wine. Mix everything and put in the oven at a medium temperature. Cook it until you see that the potatoes are golden brown.

Saltimobcca alla romana

⚒⚒⚒⚒

🕐🕐🕐🕐

💰💰💰💰

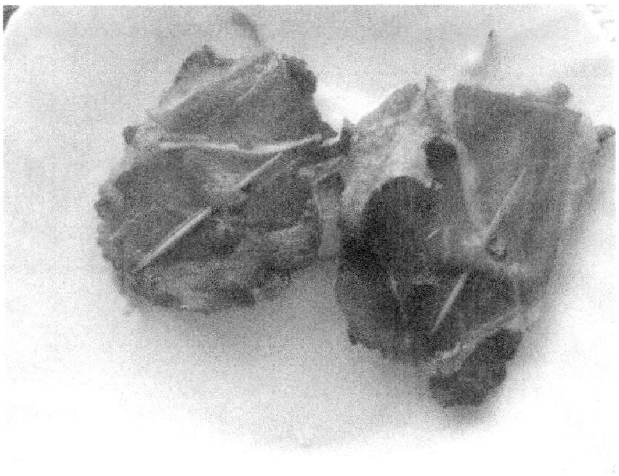

Ingredients:

- ♣ 4 slices of veal
- ♣ 50 grams of flour
- ♣ 50 grams of raw ham
- ♣ 4 bay leaves

Preparation:

Ask the butcher to cut some very thin slices of veal walnut. Flour the pieces of veal and place them neatly on a plate. Next layer the veal with slices of raw ham. Place each slice on a bay leaf and top with another slice of veal. Secure with a toothpick. Cook the saltimbocca in hot butter for a few minutes. You can also decide not flour the meat but the most important thing is to use very tender veal and cook for a few minutes.

Grilled scamorza

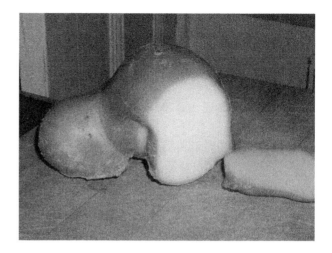

Ingredients:
* 1 smoked cheese
* 80 grams of ham

Preparation:

Cut the scamorza cheese in two pieces and place the two halves on a sheet of baking paper. Put them in the oven at the maximum temperature until they melt. Once melted, take them out of the oven and gently slide them onto the plate. While they are still hot, top with fine cut ham and serve.

Mogliia sole

❌❌❌❌
🕐🕐🕐
💰 💰 💰 💰

Ingredients:

♣ 2 fillets of sole

♣ 50 grams of butter

♣ 1 hectogram of flour

♣ 1 lemon

Preparation:

The first step is to clarify the butter. To do this, fry butter at a very low temperature. In a few minutes, you will see the butter separate into two parts, one clear and transparent and the other frothy. Gently remove the frothy part and keep the transparent part (which is good for frying without burning). Flour the sole fillets well, pressing the flour in with your hands. Put them in a pan with hot butter, brown them on both sides, and pour the lemon half over when cooked.

Beer stew

✕✕
🕐🕐🕐
💰💰💰

Ingredients:

* 400 grams of beef
* 200 ml of dark beer
* 1 tablespoon of oil
* salt and pepper to taste

Preparation:

This dish can be made in the microwave and will surely not disappoint. Cut the beef into two-centimeter cubes and put in a Pyrex dish. Add the oil and a little bit of beer. Cook in the oven at a medium temperature for 20 minutes, slowly adding the remaining beer. Serve hot with a full-bodied beer.

Meat skewers

✗✗✗
🕐🕐🕐
💰💰💰💰

Ingredients:

- 1 sausage
- 1 chicken breast
- 100 grams of veal
- 100 grams of pork pulp
- 100 ml of bacon

Preparation:

Cut all the meat into pieces of the same size and add them to large skewers, alternating the various types. Sprinkle with pepper and salt, grease with a bit of oil, and put in the oven to grill until completely cooked.

Sea bass in salt

⚒⚒

🕐🕐🕐

💰💰💰💰

Ingredients:

- ♣ 1 sea bass of 800 grams
- ♣ 1 kilo of coarse salt
- ♣ 1 clove of garlic
- ♣ ½ lemon
- ♣ 2 tablespoons of oil

Preparation:

Clean the sea bass but do not descale it. Stuff with garlic, lemon, and oil. Put a sheet of parchment paper on a baking sheet and pour half the salt on it. Put the sea bass on the paper and cover it with the remaining salt. Turn the parchment paper over so that everything is wrapped and put in the oven at maximum heat for 45 minutes. Once cooked, break up any pieces of salt, sprinkle any leftover salt, and serve.

Meat tartare

✗✗✗✗
🕐🕐🕐🕐
💰 💰 💰 💰

Ingredients:

* 300 grams of beef tenderloin
* 2 eggs
* 1 tablespoon of Worcester sauce
* 2 pinches of pepper
* 2 tablespoons of oil
* 1 lemon

Preparation:

Ask the butcher to chop the meat well. Put the meat in a bowl and add the Worcester sauce, oil, lemon juice, pepper, and a pinch of salt. Mix well with a fork and put it in the fridge to marinate for an hour. Divide the meat in two parts and use your hands to make two large meatballs. Put each in the center of a serving dish. Use your hands to make a crater in the center and add a whole shelled egg and a pinch of pepper. Serve and enjoy.

Tuna tartar

✗✗✗✗

🕐🕐🕐🕐

💰💰💰💰

Ingredients:

* 1 300-gram tuna fillet
* 1 orange
* 1 lemon
* pepper and oil

Preparation:

Buy a fresh tuna fillet and make sure it has been flash frozen. Cut it into regular-sized, small cubes. Grate one orange's peel and sprinkle it over the salmon. Next, pour over the orange juice and top with a nice handful of black pepper, half of a lemon thinly sliced, and four tablespoons of olive oil. Stir and let it rest for half an hour before serving.

Eggs with bacon

Ingredients:

- ♣ 4 eggs
- ♣ 1 hectogram of bacon
- ♣ 30 grams of butter

Preparation:

First, separate the egg whites from the yolks. Now melt the butter in a pan and, as soon as it starts to fry, add the slices of bacon. After a few moments you will see that the bacon will start to shrivel. Wait a couple of minutes and pour in the four egg whites. As soon as they begin to coagulate, add the four egg yolks. Cook for two minutes and serve.

Boiled eggs with cheese

✗✗✗

🕐🕐

💰💰

Ingredients:

- ♣ 4 eggs
- ♣ vinegar or lemon
- ♣ 4 slices
- ♣ 30 grams of grated parmesan cheese

Preparation:

Bring to a boil water water with salt and a bit of vinegar or lemon. Once boiling, turn the burner down and gently add an egg. The vinegar or lemon helps with egg white coagulation. Always boil on very low heat for three minutes. Then, with a slotted spoon, remove the egg from the water and leave it out to dry. Prepare four eggs like this and put them in an ovensafe dish. Place a thin slice on each egg, sprinkle with grated parmesan cheese and put in the oven to grill until the cheese is melted.

Boiled eggs with ham

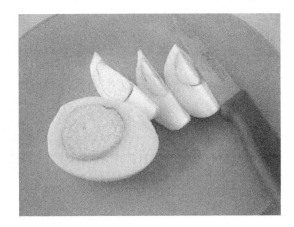

Ingredients:

* 3 eggs
* 1 hectogram of cooked ham
* 4 tablespoons of mayonnaise
* 1 tablespoon of olive oil

Preparation:

Boil the eggs in water with salt for 10 minutes. Once they start to boil, put them under running water to cool. This will help you shell them easier. Cut the eggs in half and set aside the whites. Put the egg yolks in a bowl, add the ham, oil, and mayonnaise. With a fork, chop and mix everything well. Add salt to taste and fill the egg white halves with the mixture. Put in the fridge for a half hour before serving.

Boiled eggs with truffles

Ingredients:

* 4 eggs
* 1 truffle
* 2 tablespoons of oil
* 10 grams of grated parmesan cheese

Preparation:

Boil 4 eggs in water with salt. Cool them under cool running water to make peeling easier. Cut each egg in half and mash the yolks in a bowl with a fork. Add a bit of grated truffle, two tablespoons of oil, and a little parmesan cheese. Mix everything well and pipe the mixture into the egg white halves. Sprinkle with truffle shavings and cool for half an hour in the fridge before serving.

Boiled eggs with tuna

✗✗
🕐🕐
💰 💰

Ingredients:

♣ 3 eggs

♣ 150 grams of tuna

♣ 4 tablespoons of mayonnaise

♣ 1 tablespoon of olive oil

Preparation:

Boil the eggs in water with salt for 10 minutes. Once they start boiling, put them under cool running water to make shelling easier. Cut each of the eggs in half. Put the yolks in a bowl and add the tuna, oil, and mayonnaise. Use a fork to chop and mix everything well. Add salt to taste and fill the egg white halves with this mixture. Put in the fridge for half an hour before serving.

Boiled eggs with prawns

✗✗✗
🕐🕐🕐
💰💰💰

Ingredients:

♣ 3 eggs

♣ 1 hectogram of shrimp

♣ 4 tablespoons of mayonnaise

♣ 1 tablespoon of olive oil

Preparation:

Boil the eggs in water with salt for 10 minutes. Once they start boiling, put them under cool running water to make shelling easier. Cut each of the eggs in half. Set 6 shrimp aside and add the rest to a bowl. Blend the remaining boiled and peeled shrimp with a mixer. Put the egg yolks in a bowl and add the chopped shrimp, oil, and mayonnaise. Use a fork to chop and mix well and add salt to taste. Next, fill the egg white halves with the mixture and garnish each half egg with a piece of shrimp. Put in the fridge for half an hour before serving.

Boiled eggs with sausage

✗✗✗
🕐🕐🕐
💰 💰

Ingredients:

♣ 4 eggs

♣ 2 sausages

♣ 50 grams of breadcrumbs

Preparation:

Boil four eggs and shell them. Remove the skin from two minced sausages. Spread the sausages with your hands as if it were a paste and try to wrap the hard-boiled eggs with the sausage. Next, dip the covered eggs in beaten egg and coat with breadcrumbs. Put them in a pan with oil to fry. They are ready when they are golden brown. Enjoy this delicious dish and healthy cholesterol levels!

Scrambled eggs with ham

✗✗✗

🕐🕐🕐

💰 💰

Ingredients:

♣ 4 eggs

♣ 1 hectogram of cooked ham

♣ 30 grams of butter

Preparation:

Cut the ham into small pieces. Put butter in the pan and, when it begins to fry, add the ham. Wait just a minute and add the four eggs. Use a wooden spoon to break up the eggs as they cook and scramble them well. If needed add a pinch of salt and serve.

Vitello tonnato

🛠🛠🛠🛠

🕐🕐🕐🕐

💰💰💰💰

Ingredients:

- ♣ 1 round of veal
- ♣ 400 grams of tuna
- ♣ ½ liter of white wine
- ♣ 200 grams of mayonnaise

Preparation:

Start with a half kilo round of veal. Make sure that the outside is clean using a very sharp knife. Put it in a fitting pan. Use a fork to chop 400 grams of tuna (in oil from a glass jar) and add it to the pan. Next, add a half liter of white wine, covering everything. Cover with a lid and boil on low heat for two hours. The wine needs to evaporate slowly. Be careful not to let it dry out too much. Let it rest until it is very cold, remove the from the pan and cut it into very thin slices. In the meantime, use a blender to mix the tuna until it's creamy and add the mayonnaise. Mix everything and top the cooked veal with this mixture.

the side dishes

Potato bombs

Ingredients:

- 4 potatoes
- 50 grams of Parmesan cheese
- 1 egg
- 1 pack of puff pastry
- 150 grams of mozzarella
- 100 grams of cooked ham

Preparation:

Boil four potatoes. Peel and mash them with a potato masher. Add 50 grams of grated parmesan cheese and a beaten egg. Use a rolling pin to roll the mixture out into a very thick sheet. Use a glass to make circles from the dough and set aside. Take 150 grams of mozzarella and 100 grams of cooked ham, all finely chopped. Top the potato circles with the meat and cheese. Cover and set aside. Pitch the edges well to close each circle and fry in olive oil for a few minutes.

Cacioimperio

Ingredients:

♣ 2 ounces of fontina cheese

♣ 50 grams of butter

♣ 2 egg yolks

♣ ½ liter of milk

Preparation:

Cut the fontina cheese into cubes and soak it in milk for a couple of hours. Next, drain the cheese and put it in a pan with melted butter. Stir on very low heat. Add the two egg yolks and a few spoonfuls of milk to make it soft. Plate and, if you like, top with grated truffle.

Potato croquettes

Ingredients:

- ♣ ½ kilo of potatoes
- ♣ 1 egg
- ♣ 1 hectogram of breadcrumbs
- ♣ oil

Preparation:

Boil, clean, and mash the potatoes with a potato masher or a fork. Salt the potatoes and, with your hands, roll out 5 centimeters long "snakes". Dip in beaten egg and coat with breadcrumbs. Fry in pletly of oil and serve.

Boiled potatos

✗✗

⏱⏱⏱

💰

Ingredients:

♣ 1 kilo of potatoes

♣ sauces to your liking

Preparation:

Though simple, boiled potatos are a real delicacy. You can use this dish as a base and add a wide variety of sauces. The possibilities are endless. Start with potatoes that are all same size (so that the cooking time is consistent). Boil them until a toothpick enters the potato perfectly and effortlessly. Strain and peel them while hot. Cut them into large slices or, if you prefer, into pieces and season to your liking. A simple and classic topping is oil, salt, and pepper. Another favorite is truffle sauce or even cold with mayonnaise. If you want to top them with canned tuna (from a glass container), always serve cold and cut into small pieces. Another way to prepare this dish is to mix the potatoes with yogurt and spices to your liking. You can also mix them with small pieces of smoked provola and speck (bacon). Another variant is to replace the speck (bacon) with smoked salmon. As you can see, there are many delicious ways to prepare boiled potatoes.

Potatoes and bacon

✄✄✄
🕐🕐🕐
💰 💰

Ingredients:

♣ 4 potatoes

♣ 1 hectogram of bacon

♣ pepper

Preparation:

Peel four nice potatoes and cut them into pieces. Boil them in water with salt until they are soft enough. They should not boil completely but must be blanched. Strain and put in a Pryex dish. Add one hundred grams of cubbed bacon and mix with a wooden spoon. Cook it in the oven at a high temperature until a crust forms. Add salt to taste and serve.

Mashed potatoes

Ingredients:

♣ ½ kilo of potatoes

♣ 20 grams of butter

Preparation:

Boil one half kilo of potatoes. Peel and mash them and add one hundred grams of warm milk, 20 grams of butter at room temperature, and a nice handful of parmesan cheese. Mix well with a wooden spoon and serve. To flavor, you can add cream and a sprinkle of nutmeg.

Ricotta au gratin

✗✗✗

🕐🕐🕐

💰 💰

Ingredients:

- ♣ 200 grams of ricotta
- ♣ 500 grams of flour
- ♣ ½ glass of milk
- ♣ 2 tablespoons of grated parmesan cheese
- ♣ 20 grams of ham
- ♣ 20 grams of butter
- ♣ 1 egg

Preparation:

Add the flour and egg to a bowl and mix with a wooden spoon. Add the ricotta and dilute it with milk. Next, add the parmesan and chopped ham. Grease a Pyrex dish with your hands, pour in the mixture, and put it in the oven. When it starts to brown, take out of the oven, and serve.

Potato flan

✕✕✕

🕐🕐🕐🕐

⏳ ⏳

Ingredients:

- ♣ 50 grams of butter
- ♣ 1 kilo of potatoes
- ♣ 1 hectogram of cooked ham
- ♣ 3 eggs
- ♣ 1 mozzarella of 125 grams
- ♣ 30 grams of butter
- ♣ 50 grams of Parmesan cheese

Preparation:

Carefully grease a Pyrex dish with butter. In the meantime, boil a kilo of potatoes. Once you can easily insert, take the potatoes off the burner. Peel them while hot and mash coarsely with a fork. Add a beaten egg, one hundred grams of cooked ham (often cut into small pieces), two hard-boiled eggs cut into slices, one hundred grams of mozzarella, one piece of nutmeg grated, 50 grams of butter cut small pieces at room temperature, and 50 grams of grated parmesan cheese. Mix everything carefully and pour into the Pyrex dish. Mash with a fork and put in the oven for half an hour. Then, grill for few minutes to brown the top. It is a heavy dish that can be eaten hot or cold.

desserts and sweets

Bananas flambé

✗ ✗ ✗

🕐 🕐

💰 💰

Ingredients:

- ♣ 2 bananas
- ♣ ½ glass of rum
- ♣ 1 orange
- ♣ 30 grams of butter
- ♣ brown sugar to taste

Preparation:

Pour the orange juice into a Pyrex dish and put it on the burner to heat. As soon as it begins to caramelize, add the butter. Clean the bananas and cut them lengthwise. Add them to the Pyrex dish to cook, turning them several times. Next, add the rum, or, if you prefer, another liqueur can also be used. Let the liqueur catch fire for a few seconds. Without breaking them, plate the bananas and add the syrup from the pan on top. Serve warm.

Cream puffs

⚒⚒⚒

🕐🕐🕐

💰💰

Ingredients:

♣ 120 grams of water ♣ 75 grams of 00 flour ♣ 60 grams of butter♣ 2 eggs ♣ 1 pinch of salt ♣ 2 egg yolks ♣ 60 grams of sugar ♣ 30 grams of 00 flour ♣ 125 ml of whole milk ♣ 125 ml of cream ♣ grated lemon zest ♣ ½ vanilla bean ♣ powered sugar for finishing

Preparation: Boil the water, butter, and salt in a pyrex bowl. Turn off the burner and add the sifted flour (all at once). Mix with a whisk. Turn the burner back on and cook, stirring with a wooden spoon until the mixture has thickened. Put the mixture in a bowl and let it cool. Use an electric mixer to incorporate the eggs, one at a time. Continue until you have a mixture that is smooth. Put the mixture into a pastry bag with a 15 mm nozzle. Use this to form small balls of dough on a baking sheet lined with parchment paper. Put the baking sheet in the oven (preheated to 180 degrees) for about 25 to 30 minutes. Take it out of the oven and let it cool to room temperature. In a Pyrex bowl, mix the egg yolks with the sugar using a whisk. Gradually add the flour and mix until the mixture is homogeneous. Gradually pour in the boiling milk and cream with a pinch of vanilla and a bit of grated lemon peel. Put the dish on the stove to warm, continuing to stir, and simmer for 3-4 minutes. Now add the cream to bowl and let it cool. Put the cream in a pastry bag with a small nozzle and use it to fill the cupcakes by making a small hole in the bottom. Sprinkle with powdered sugar and serve.

Fig biscuits -

⚒⚒⚒⚒

🕐🕐🕐

💰💰

Ingredients:

- 120 grams of honey
- 6 tablespoons of apple juice
- 4 tablespoons of orange juice
- 350 grams of dried figs
- 40 grams of pine nuts
- 2 teaspoons of grated lemon zest
- 460 grams of flour
- qb grams of flour for processing
- 100 grams of sugar
- ¼ tablespoon of salt
- 2 eggs
- 6 tablespoons of milk

Preparation:

Coarsely chop the figs and pine nuts. Heat the figs, pine nuts, honey, and orange juice in a Pyrex bowl. Add the lemon zest and let it cool. Put the flour, sugar, and salt in a blender. Once blended, add the eggs, and mix. Once blended, transfer it to a floured surface. Work the dough with your hands, wrap it in plastic wrap, and put it in the fridge to chill for 40 minutes. Next, roll out the dough until you have a square measuring about 20 centimeters on each side. Next, add the fig/nut mixture to the center of the dough, making a long strip. Moisten the edges of the dough with a little water and bring the edges together to form a roll. Now, cut the roll into logs measuring a few centimeters. Put the logs in a baking dish and cook at 180 degrees for 20 minutes. Take out of the oven, cool, and sprinkle with powered sugar.

Creme caramel

✗✗
🕐🕐🕐
💰 💰 💰

Ingredients:

♣450 grams of milk,♣ 120 grams of sugar,♣ one egg yolk, ♣♣another four eggs, ♣150 grams of cream.

Preparation:

Pour the milk into a bowl and bring it to a boil. Once it reaches a boil, turn off and leave to infuse for half an hour. After this time, mix and keep aside for a moment. In a separate bowl, beat the eggs with the sugar. At this point slowly pour in the milk and cream mixture, filtering it through a sieve then stir again with a whisk to obtain a homogeneous mixture. Distribute the mixture obtained inside with the help of a ladle. Pour boiling water into the pan to cover a third of the molds. Then cook in a bain-marie for about 50 minutes. Once cooked, leave to cool and transfer the molds to the refrigerator to cool for at least 4 hours. After the cooling time has elapsed, unmold the caramel creams using the blade of a small knife to better detach from the edges and serve

Crepes with butter and sugar

✗✗✗✗

🕐🕐

💰 💰

Ingredients:

♣ 150 grams of flour

♣ 2 eggs

♣ 25 cl of milk

♣ salt

♣ oil

Preparation:

Add the flour to a large bowl and make a crater in the middle. Break the eggs into this crater and mix slowly. Add the milk and mix well so that the mixture does not form lumps. Add the oil and salt, mix well, and set aside for 1 hour at room temperature. Pour half a ladle of dough into a hot pan and cook until the edges come up (about 30 sec). Flip and cook on the other side. Plate and top with butter and sprinkle with sugar.

Fruit tart without cooking

✗✗✗

🕐🕐🕐🕐

💰 💰

Ingredients:

- ♣ 150 grams of cookies
- ♣ 50 grams of butter
- ♣ 1 tablespoon of honey
- ♣ 1 hectogram of fresh cream
- ♣ 1 hectogram of cream cheese
- ♣ 40 grams of powdered sugar
- ♣ fresh fruit to taste

Preparation:

Put the biscuits, honey, and butter in a mixer and blend well until it forms a powder. Press the mixture into a mold making sure to cover the bottom and sides of each mold. Put it in the fridge for thirty minutes. While the crust is cooling, prepare the cream. Add the cream, cream cheese, and sugar to a Pyrex bowl. Mix it well with a whisk until it is creamy and smooth. Remove the mold from the fridge, pour in the cream, and cover with the fresh fruit (washed and cut). Put in the fridge for an hour before serving.

Sweet chestnut fruit tart

✗ ✗ ✗ ✗

🕐 🕐 🕐

💰 💰

Ingredients:

* 150 grams of flour
* 80 grams of butter
* 80 grams of sugar
* 2 eggs
* 1 lemon
* various fruit: grapes, strawberries, oranges, mandarins ...

Preparation:

Mix the flour, butter, 40 grams of sugar, an egg yolk, and the grated lemon and let it rest for a couple of hours. Beat an egg yolk with the remaining sugar in a saucepan on very low heat until a soft cream is formed. Grease a baking tray and cover the tray with the dough. Bake in the oven for half an hour, then pour the cream on top, and add the chopped fruit.

Dessert with Chestnuts

Ingredients:

♣ 2 eggs

♣ 50 grams of vanilla sugar

♣ 15 grams of flour

♣ 200 grams of cream

♣ 15 grams of butter

♣ 4 ounces of chestnuts

♣ 1 liter of milk

♣ 1 hectogram of sugar

Preparation:

We will start by making the custard. Mix the egg yolks with the sugar and flour. Add the cream and cook over very low heat. Cut the shell of each of the chestnuts and boil them in the milk for an hour. Once the chestnuts are cooked, set aside a few whole chestnuts, and puree the rest. Mix the chestnut puree with the sugar and a quarter of the custard. Plate the chestnut puree and cover with the custard. Garnish with the remaining whole chestnuts.

Pan di spagna

⚒⚒⚒

🕐🕐

💰💰💰

Ingredients:

- ♣ 75 grams of flour
- ♣ 3 eggs
- ♣ 1 hectogram of sugar
- ♣ butter to taste

Preparation:

Separate the egg yolks and whites and put in two different bowls. Use a whisk to mix the egg yolks with the sugar until a frothy cream is formed. Beat the egg whites until stiff. Add the whipped eggs whites to the mixture prepared with egg yolks and sugar. Add the well-sifted flour slowly to make sure the mixture doesn't come apart. When the mixture is homogeneous pour it into a 15cm baking pan that has been greased and floured. Put it in the oven at 180 degrees and let it cook for 40 minutes. Before taking the sponge cake out of the oven, let it rest for 10 minutes.

Panna cotta

✕✕✕
🕐🕐
💰💰💰

Ingredients:

- ♣ 200 grams of cream
- ♣ 4 sheets of gelatin
- ♣ 40 grams of sugar
- ♣ 1 vile of vanilla flavoring

Preparation:

Melt the gelatine and leave it in cold water. Add it to a Pyrex bowl and mix in the cream, sugar, and vanilla. Mix well and put on the stove at low temperature. Be sure to stir constantly and, as soon as it starts to boil, turn off the burner.

Wet the molds with cold water and pour in the mixture. Refrigerate for at least 4 hours before serving.

Panna cotta can be eaten plain or can be garnished with many different kinds of fruit.

American cake

🛠🛠🛠🛠

🕐🕐🕐🕐

💰💰💰💰

Ingredients:

- ♣ ½ kilo of sweet potatoes
- ♣ 2 tablespoons of sugar
- ♣ 1 egg
- ♣ breadcrumbs
- ♣ cinnamon

Preparation:

Boil the potatoes in water with sugar. Drain them well and mash them in the potato masher. Add the cinnamon, sugar, and an egg yolk and mix. Pour the mixture into a greased pan sprinkled with breadcrumbs. Spread the beaten egg whites on top and put in the oven on medium heat.

Apple pie with ricotta

✗✗✗✗
🕐🕐🕐🕐
💰 💰

. Ingredients:
- ♣ 1 hectogram of ricotta
- ♣ 2 discs of sponge cake
- ♣ 15 grams of honey
- ♣ 2 apples
- ♣ 1 lemon
- ♣ 30 grams of powdered sugar

Preparation:

Mix the ricotta with the powdered sugar, lemon juice, and vanilla. Cut 1 ½ apples into cubes and cook on medium heat with honey. Mix the ricotta with the apple cubes and set aside. Put a circular piece of sponge cake on a tray and top with the ricotta and apple mixture. Cover with another circular piece of sponge cake and garnish the top with the sliced apples and brown sugar or powered sugar to taste.

Apple cake

✕✕✕✕

🕐🕐🕐🕐

💰 💰

Ingredients:

♣ ½ kilo of honey

♣ 125 grams of flour

♣ 2 eggs

♣ 60 grams of sugar

♣ ¼ of milk

♣ 1 lemon

Preparation:

Slowly beat the eggs with the sugar in a bowl. Slowly add the flour, grated lemon peel, and a little bit of milk to make a thick cream. Coat a baking sheet with butter. Add the apple cut into very thin slices and top with the cream mixture. Sprinkle with sugar and put in the oven on medium heat to bake.

Apple and cheese pie

⚒⚒⚒⚒

🕐🕐🕐🕐

💰💰

Ingredients:

♣ 2 golden apples

♣ 40 grams of sugar

♣ 25 grams of butter

♣ 70 grams of biscuits

♣ 1 sachet of gelatin

♣ 250 grams of cream

Preparation:

Peel and core the applies and cut thme into slices. In a saucepan, heat 20 g of butter on low heat without bringing it to a boil. Add the apple slices and cook until soft. Pour in 40 g of sugar and let the caramel cover the fruit until the fruit is a golden color. Remove from the burner and set aside. Melt 30 g of butter and it in a bowl with the biscuits broken into pieces. Mix until homogenous. Cover the bottom of a circular baking pan with the mixture. Next, boil the cream, 40 g of sugar, and the quark cheese. Add gelatin to the mixture. Pour into the mold and leave to cool in the refrigerator for 6 hours. Remove the cake from the refrigerator and cover it with the apple slices in a circle design. Carefully take the cake out of the mold and serve.

Tartar pie

✗ ✗ ✗ ✗

🕐 🕐 🕐 🕐

💰 💰 💰

Ingredients:

* 1 hectogram of ricotta
* 2 ounces of jam
* 1 glass of brandy
* 150 grams of ladyfinger biscuits
* 20 grams of powdered sugar
* 1 spoonful of cream

Preparation:

Mix the cream with the ricotta and butter. Coat a cake pan with liqueur and make a layer of biscuits at the bottom. Sprinkle with brandy and cover with jam. Make another layer of biscuits and cover it with the ricota mixture. Conntinue to make other layers and then put in the refrigerator to chill.

Printed in Great Britain
by Amazon

39170609R00106